Tom, Dick and Harry

A Comedy

Ray and Michael Cooney

A Samuel French Acting Edition

SAMUEL FRENCH

FOUNDED 1830

SAMUELFRENCH-LONDON.CO.UK
SAMUELFRENCH.COM

TOM, DICK AND HARRY

First performed at the Theatre Royal, Windsor on 21st October 2003 with the following cast.

Tom Kerwood	Bradley Walsh
Linda Kerwood	Jenny Funnell
Dick Kerwood	Joe Pasquale
Harry Kerwood	Richard Gauntlett
Katerina	Sarah Wateridge
Andreas	Royce Mills
Constable Downs	Jeffrey Holland
Mrs Potter	Louise Jameson
Boris	David Warwick

Directed by Ray Cooney
Designed by Douglas Heap

Subsequently produced by Ray Cooney Presentations at the Duke of York's Theatre, London on 10th August, 2005, with the following cast.

Tom Kerwood	Joe McGann
Linda Kerwood	Hannah Waterman
Dick Kerwood	Stephen McGann
Harry Kerwood	Mark McGann
Andreas	Brian Greene
Katerina	Sarah Wateridge
Constable Downs	Mark Wingett
Mrs Potter	Louise Jameson
Boris	David Warwick

Directed by Ray Cooney
Designed by Douglas Heap

CHARACTERS
(In order of appearance)

Tom Kerwood is a likeable Londoner in his late twenties/ early thirties.

Linda Kerwood is in her late twenties, attractive, bright and sparky.

Dick Kerwood is a lovable rogue.

Harry Kerwood is a genius, but thick.

Katerina is a Kosovan in her late twenties/early thirties, a poorly dressed peasant, buxom and attractive. She is confident and dangerous.

Andreas is a small eighty-year-old shabby Kosovan, stooped and weather-beaten.

Constable Downs is a homely officer in his mid-forties.

Mrs Potter is a formidable lady in her early fifties.

Boris is a stocky East-European about forty. Very smartly dressed.

SYNOPSIS OF SCENES

The action of the play takes place in the Kennington home of Tom and Linda Kerwood in London.

ACT I   The morning of a bright spring day
ACT II Immediately following

Time—the present

AUTHORS' NOTE

The play is set in London and the immigrants have arrived from Kosovo via Calais. However, if any production outside the UK preferred to set it in their own territory with the immigrants arriving from a more appropriate country, this would be completely acceptable.

In this printed version of the script when Katerina, Andreas and Boris speak Albanian, their dialogue is written in phonetical Albanian, followed by English [in brackets] and then the Albanian translation in capitals.

Ray and Michael Cooney

Also by Michael Cooney
published by Samuel French

Cash on Delivery

Other plays by Ray Cooney
published by Samuel French

Caught in the Net
Funny Money
It Runs in the Family
Out of Order
Run for Your Wife
Two Into One
Why Not Stay for Breakfast? (*with Gene Stone*)
Wife Begins at Forty (*with Arne Sultan and Ray Barrett*)

ACT I

The flat of Tom and Linda Kerwood in Kennington, London. 9.05 a.m. on a bright spring day and the time advances with the action of the play

It is a two-storey Edwardian house converted into two flats. The front door is in the rear wall. L of this are stairs leading up to a landing and then a few more stairs leading UL to a door—through which is Dick Kerwood's flat. The door leading to the kitchen is UL in the L wall and below this is a window (with a ledge about three feet from the floor) through which can be seen the back garden. The door to the bedroom is UR in the R wall and the door to the dining-room is DR. Although the house is clearly Edwardian the décor is working-class, tastefully modern. There is a sofa-bed DRC. There is a table L of the sofa-bed and on it is the hands-free telephone. An armchair is DLC, with a small table to its right. There is a desk against the rear wall UR and coat hooks to the R of the front door. There is a practical clock on the wall which, when the curtain rises, shows the time at five past nine. The clock continues to show the time moving forward throughout the act and is referred to by Tom and Linda throughout the first act. As the action is continuous the Stage Management must remember to accommodate the interval!!

The CURTAIN *rises on an empty stage*

Linda Kerwood enters from the bedroom and crosses to the kitchen. She is in her late twenties, attractive, bright and sparky. She is wearing the skirt of a suit and a blouse and carrying an official looking document with a pen

Linda (*stopping, calling back towards the bedroom*) Saucepan handles!

Tom Kerwood enters from the bedroom. He is a likeable Londoner in his late twenties/early thirties. At the moment he is wearing the trousers of a suit, socks and shoes and drying his hair with a towel

Both he and Linda are clearly excited and nervous

Tom What was that one?
Linda Saucepan handles!
Tom OK. Saucepan handles must be turned inwards. Turned inwards at all times. Yeah?

Linda Very good!

She ticks a box on the document and exits into the kitchen

(*As she goes*) "Electrical equipment."

Tom (*calling into the kitchen*) Ah, this is the one I know by heart. "Keep electrical equipment inaccessible to small children and put away all appliances immediately after use — preferably in a cupboard fitted with a child-proof safety lock!" Ta-ra! (*He sits on the sofa-bed*)

Linda enters

Linda First aid kit?

Tom (*smugly*) We have two first aid kits, Linda. One is in *our* bathroom and the other's upstairs in Dick's flat.

Linda Full marks, Tom. You know all the rules!

She sits beside him on the sofa-bed and snuggles up

(*Nonchalantly*) So — are you doing anything special today?

Tom (*casually*) No, not really. How about you?

Linda Nope.

Tom (*still off-hand*) So, why have you taken a day off from the office?

Linda Why aren't you on the building site wearing your funny hat carrying a load of bricks?

Tom (*casually*) I'm adopting a baby, that's all.

Linda (*casually*) Oh, yeah? I'm adopting a baby, too.

Tom (*casually*) Oh, yeah.

There is a slight pause and then they suddenly yell in delight

Tom }
Linda } (*together*) We're adopting a baby!

They laugh and hug. A kettle whistles from the kitchen

Linda Right. Quick cup of tea. What time is it?

She goes into the kitchen

Tom Five past nine. God! Only fifty-five minutes before that woman arrives.(*Calling out*) What's her name again?

Linda (*off*) Mrs Potter.

Tom Yeah. Mrs Potter. (*A la Red Indian*) Heap Big Chief Adoption Agency. (*Calling into the kitchen, still à la Red Indian*) If Mrs Potter no like Mr and Mrs Kerwood, Mrs Potter scalp 'em!

Linda enters with two mugs of tea, closing the kitchen door

Linda (*seriously*) God, I hope she does approve us, Tom.
Tom (*grinning*) She will! She'll love us.

He exits into the bedroom

Linda puts down the two mugs of tea on the L table and moves towards the bedroom door

Linda But she's the top person. Everything depends on this interview. The rest of our lives depends on it. Some little baby's life.

Tom enters putting on his shirt

Tom Look, everyone else at the Agency thinks we're great. We've been through all the tests. Mrs Potter just wants to check we're going to give the baby a stable home.
Linda What if she doesn't like the house? I feel sick, Tom.
Tom The house is great.
Linda But we only rent it. That was one of the first questions. Do you own your own home?
Tom Well, that's what we're planning to do, aren't we? We've made the old boy an offer and he's considering it.
Linda We've made the old boy half a dozen offers and he's turned them all down.
Tom We're going to make another one though, aren't we? He's already given us the go-ahead to build that conservatory in the garden. And don't forget we sub-let the top floor. Bit of extra income. All Brownie points for us.
Linda (*somewhat comforted*) Yes, I suppose so. (*Suddenly*) Hey, where *is* that layabout brother of yours? I haven't seen him this morning. (*She goes up the stairs*)
Tom Probably still in bed.
Linda I don't want him around when Mrs Potter arrives. (*She bangs on the flat door and then pushes it open. Calling up*) Dick! You up yet, you lazy bugger!
Tom Come to think of it I haven't seen him since Friday when he borrowed the van.

Linda (*coming downstairs*) He's probably kipping with some girl-friend.
Tom Lucky sod!

Tom goes into the bedroom

She jokingly throws one of the cushions from the chair after him

Linda (*calling through*) Well, if you see him before I do tell him to keep out
of the way while Mrs Potter's here.
Tom (*off*) Right.
Linda A couple of his dirty jokes and she wouldn't let us adopt a stray cat.
Tom (*off*) OK, OK.
Linda And tell him to pay us the back rent he owes us!

Tom enters, now putting on a tie

Tom All right. (*Indicating his tie*) Do this for me, will you?
Linda (*starting to tie his tie*) What a family!
Tom Now don't start on that again!
Linda Well, Harry's just as bad.
Tom Harry's OK. Got his own place now.
Linda So why does he doss down on our sofa-bed (*pointing*) two or three
times a week?
Tom Be fair. You know that's only because his landlady won't let him in the
house when he's drunk.
Linda Useless!
Tom At least he's working. Made a big success at St Thomas's.
Linda He's the third assistant hospital porter.
Tom He'll go on from there.
Linda He started off as the first assistant hospital porter. I can't believe the
three of you are from the same gene pool.
Tom (*grinning*) But Dick and Harry are from the shallow end.
Linda (*finishing tying his tie*) There! Now — ! (*She looks around*) Have we
forgotten anything?
Tom No. It's all going to be OK.

He pulls her to him

Linda Yeah. Piece of cake.
Tom "Cake and sweets should be limited to three small snacks a day and
never be used as emotional bribery."

They laugh and kiss

Linda Oo! Flowers!
Tom "Flowers must never have thorny stems or poisonous leaves."
Linda No! I didn't get flowers!
Tom Not to panic, love. I'll pop round to Tesco's. Plenty of time.
Linda I'll go. You finish dressing. And do your hair. I'll grab my purse.

As she moves to go to the bedroom the doorbell goes

Can't be Mrs Potter, surely. (*She looks at the clock*) Fifty minutes early.

They both take a deep breath and prepare themselves. Linda opens the front door

Dick breezily walks in. He is a lovable rogue. He kisses Linda on the cheek

Dick Hi sweetheart, forgot the key.
Linda Oh, it's you.
Dick Now is that a nice way to greet a family member?
Linda You're not my family, you're his.

She points to Tom and goes into the bedroom

Dick (*calling after her*) Any tea going?
Linda (*off*) No, there isn't!

Dick sprawls on the sofa-bed

Tom It's a busy morning, Dick. The lady from the adoption agency is coming at ten.
Dick Just think. There's some lucky little kid gonna get me for an uncle.
Tom I don't think we'll advertise that. We're hoping to finalize it today.

Linda returns with her handbag

Linda Praying, you mean. (*To Dick*) And you keep out of the way. (*She is checking in her bag for her purse*)
Dick No problem. Just wanted to say thanks for the loan of the van and return the keys.

Dick gives Tom the keys to the van. Linda has found her purse. She gives Tom a quick kiss

Linda Right, Won't be long. (*To Tom*) Do your hair! (*To Dick*) And you!

Dick Yes, darling?
Linda You're three weeks late with your rent.
Dick (*to Tom*) Haven't I paid this month's rent yet?
Linda (*flatly*) You're three weeks late with last month's rent.
Dick Time flies, doesn't it? I'll write you a cheque today.
Linda And sign it this time will you?

She exits through the front door

Dick The sister-in-law from hell.
Tom Oy, oy, oy!!

Tom exits into the bedroom

Dick So how much do I owe for the loan of the van?

Dick rises, picks up Linda's mug of tea and sits in the armchair DLC

Tom enters rubbing gel into his hair

Tom You're family, you daft bugger.
Dick No, I insist. I had it a whole weekend and I'll do very well out of it.
Tom How do you mean? You were only helping a mate to move furniture, weren't you?
Dick Is that what I said?
Tom To his new flat.
Dick No, he can do that any old time. I went to Calais for the weekend.
Tom (*surprised*) Calais? What, in my van.
Dick Yeah.
Tom Why'd you need my van in Calais?
Dick To bring back the cigarettes. (*He sips the tea*)
Tom Richard — you haven't been doing anything illegal, have you?
Dick Nah. Customs are far too busy to worry about a few fags in the back of a van.
Tom How many fags?
Dick I don't know the exact number.
Tom Roughly.
Dick (*shrugging*) Two hundred.
Tom (*surprised*) You went all the way to Calais for two hundred fags?
Dick Well, no.
Tom Two hundred packets?
Dick Well, no.
Tom Well, two hundred what? Cartons.

Dick Two hundred "boxes".

Tom How many are there in a box?

Dick What, cigarettes, packets or cartons?

Tom Cigarettes! How many cigarettes in the packets in the cartons in the two hundred bloody boxes?!

Dick Well, let's see, each box contains (*he mumbles something*) cartons and each carton contains (*he mumbles something*) packets. Twenty in a packet — four hundred thousand cigarettes.

Tom (*agog*) You have smuggled four hundred thousand fags through customs?

Dick All for my own use, mate.

Tom Are you mad!

Dick (*chuckling*) It's a doddle. A couple of Boot Sales this Sunday and they'll be gone.

Tom Well, get 'em up to your flat, bloody quick. (*He thrusts the van keys at Dick*)

Dick No listen. It's my turn to do you a favour. You're going to have an extra mouth to feed, aren't you? Right. I'm giving you half the proceeds from the fags for the loan of the van.

Tom I don't want *any* of the proceeds!

Dick How about a crate of brandy?

Tom I don't want ... You didn't ... ?! You did! How many crates?

Dick Only half a dozen. You've got to get a bigger van.

Tom You cheeky bugger! Linda will hit the roof if she finds out. Get 'em upstairs quick!

He pushes Dick towards the front door and opens it

Harry is standing there. He's wearing hospital overalls and carrying four full Sainsbury's shopping bags. Harry is a genius — but thick

Harry (*to Tom*) Big brother! (*To Dick*) Medium brother!

Dick (*to Harry*) Little brother!

Tom Both brothers, bugger off. Sorry, Harry, but this is not a good time. The lady's coming from the Adoption Agency at ten o'clock.

Harry strolls past Tom and puts the bags down downstage of the sofa-bed

Harry (*interrupting*) I know. That's why I'm here. I've come to do you a big favour, mate.

Tom (*pointedly*) I'm not in the market for favours today.

Harry You'll love this. (*To Dick*) He'll love this.

Tom I won't.

Dick I might quite like it.
Harry No, this is for big brother only. (*He sits Tom*) Now. You want to own
your own home, don't you?
Tom Harry —— !

Tom tries to stand up, Harry sits him

Harry (*pressing on*) No, you're gonna love me for this. (*To Dick*) He's going
to love me.

Dick sits beside them

Dick (*to Tom*) You're gonna love him. (*To Harry*) Let's hear it.
Harry (*to Tom*) Are you and Linda still interested in buying this house?
Tom Harry, we've been through all this. The owner wants a fortune.
Harry How much?
Tom Three hundred grand at least. (*To Dick*) Will you get those cigarettes
upstairs!
Harry (*interested*) Cigarettes?
Dick I did the Calais run.
Harry No problems?
Dick No problems.
Harry I can shift some for you.
Dick And the brandy?
Harry Easy peasy.
Tom Hey, do you mind!
Harry Sorry. About the house ——

Tom rises

Tom (*interrupting*) I don't want to know about the house. (*To Dick*) I want
you to clear out my van. (*To Harry*) And I want you to clear off.

Dick sits Tom

Dick No rush. (*To Harry*) Give.
Harry (*to Tom, pleased with himself*) What would you say if I told you I
could get this house for less than £200,000?
Tom I'd say you'd been sniffing formaldehyde at the hospital morgue.
Dick (*to Tom, chuckling*) Very good, Tommy. (*To Harry*) What's formal-
dehyde?
Harry (*to Tom*) I've got an ingenious scheme.
Tom I've told you. I'm not getting involved in any more of your schemes.

Harry This is sure fire.
Tom (*to Dick*) That's what he said about all that French wine. I've still got five hundred litres of the stuff in the garden shed.
Dick Well, how was he to know that "Vin de Aigre" was French for vinegar.
Harry Yes, you can't win 'em all. But, this one —! Take a butcher's at this.

Harry produces a sheaf of papers. Tom sighs and grabs it

Tom (*impatiently*) It's a list of properties.
Harry Yeah. Houses for sale in this area. You can't get anything halfway decent for less than two hundred and eighty-five thousand round here, can you?
Tom I know! That's why the old boy keeps turning us down.
Harry (*pointing*) Look at that one!
Tom (*reading*) "26 Becton Street."
Harry Three bedroom semi, two full baths, new kitchen, nice size garden —
Tom (*interrupting tersely*) Yeah, it sounds lovely.
Harry Now look at the price.

Tom does so; his eyes widen

Dick Becton Street — rings a bell.
Tom (*reading, amazed*) A hundred and sixty thousand.

He looks up at Harry who grins triumphantly. Dick snatches the sheaf of papers and inspects it

Tom (*to Harry*) What's wrong with the place?
Harry Nothing. It's a corker.
Dick Wait a minute. Becton Street. Didn't something horrible happen there?
Harry It certainly did. A couple of years ago. "The Butcher of Becton Street".
Dick Right! A nice young couple bought the place and then found lots of mangled bodies buried in the garden.
Harry It was only two bodies. They found lots of mangled bits and pieces.

Tom is looking from one to the other in disbelief

Dick And they couldn't identify any of them because they were mangled years ago and whoever did it mangled them into such tiny pieces ——
Tom (*interrupting*) Hang on, hang on, hang on! (*To Harry*) Linda and I don't want to live in a place like that!

Harry No, no. I'm using this as an example. The young couple are now selling and the house price is ludicrous because of the gruesome murders. That's where I got the idea from.

Tom *(flatly)* What idea, Harry?

Harry No listen, it's my turn to do you a favour. I saw how upset you were when you couldn't find the cash for a deposit on this place. Linda, especially. So when I saw this …

Dick Cut to the chase will you.

Harry *(to Dick)* No, he's going to love me for this. *(To Tom)* You're going to love me.

Tom Get on with it!

Harry OK. I work at St Thomas's hospital, don't I? Now! A couple of days a week I do morgue duty. What if I got my hands on a cadaver. A dead body!

Tom just stares at him

You know, something the students had had a go at — and we buried it under your patio! *(He points to the window DL)* Now, Alfie Frost and the boys start next week on your new conservatory, don't they? They'll dig up the body — "Oh my Gawd! Panic! Police, what have you … !" — the price of the house will plummet — and you and Linda will easily be able to borrow the money for a deposit.

Harry is very pleased with himself. Tom looks blankly to Dick and back to Harry — then bursts out laughing and looks to Dick to join in. He looks back to Harry

Tom *(suddenly stopping)* You're serious, aren't you? *(To Dick)* He's serious!

Dick It's a bloody good idea, isn't it?!

Tom *(rising)* Are you mad? You're criminal maniacs! Where the hell do you get it from?

Dick Dad would have thought it was a bloody good idea, too.

Tom *(to Dick)* You with your four hundred thousand cigarettes. *(To Harry)* You with your Godiva!

Harry "Cadaver."

Tom Shut up! You're both a bloody disgrace to the Kerwood family.

Dick Hey, you've done the odd dodgy deed in your time.

Tom All right but I've seen the error of my ways, haven't I? Now you get those fags sorted out and then go for a long walk.

He pushes Dick to the front door

Dick OK, OK. Here, Harry. How do you get hold of this formaldehyde stuff?

Tom Get out!

Dick goes

Harry I'm sorry you feel like this.
Tom Look, I'm grateful, Harry. I know you were trying to help me and Linda.
But next time come up with something that won't result in a lengthy prison
sentence, yeah?
Harry I don't see how anything could go wrong.
Tom Funny, that's what Crippen said. You get back to the hospital. I'll give
you a buzz and let you know how we get on about the baby.
Harry Yeah. Good luck. Be great having a little babby-doo about the house.
There's just one thing?
Tom Yeah?
Harry What'll I do with the body?

*There is a pause as Tom takes this in. He then eases the door to—but not shut
— and marches Harry* DC

Tom (*flatly*) Body?
Harry The cadaver from the hospital.
Tom (*in disbelief*) The cad ... You don't mean ... ? No, you haven't actually
taken a body?
Harry That was the plan.
Tom (*suddenly shouting*) There *was* no plan! (*Quickly pulling himself
together*) OK, OK. You're my brother (*To himself*) Deal with it, Tom.
Steady, steady. Harry — how did you get this body out of the hospital?
Harry Boot of my car.
Tom (*controlling himself*) Boot of your car. OK.
Harry In a heavy duty bin bag.
Tom Heavy duty, yeah, would be.
Harry Look, the bloke's dead. It's only a dead body.
Tom (*still in control*) Only a dead body ... Yep. Bloke's dead. Where's your
car, Harry?
Harry Outside the front of your house. Parked behind your white van.
Tom (*still managing to be in control*) Behind my white — uh-huh. OK. Your
car is outside my house parked behind my white van and in your car boot
is a heavy duty bin bag and in the bin bag is a dead body, yeah?
Harry No. The car is parked outside the front but the bin bag with the body
is in your back garden.

Harry indicates the window DL. *Tom looks slowly towards the window*

I dropped the body off first then drove round the front so we could discuss
the *modus operandi*.

Tom (*suddenly cracking*) Are you mental?! You great big … ! God! (*He smacks his head*) Today of all … ! You … ! I've got Mrs Potter … ! You … A dead … ! In my … ! I'm adopting a … ! You … ! (*He starts to punch the cushions on the chair* DLC)

Harry I've never seen you so aggressive before, Tom.

Tom Stick around, you … ! (*He marches past Harry and leans his head on the dining-room door*)

Harry (*simply*) He's definitely dead if that's what's worrying you.

Tom (*yelling in anguish*) Ahhh!

Tom bangs his head on the door as:

Dick enters from the front door struggling with a huge heavy unmarked box

Dick Hey, you two better help with these ——

Tom Ahhhh!!

Dick (*to Harry*) What's the matter with him?

Harry He didn't like the idea.

Tom (*to Dick, pointing at Harry*) This — tit — has got a body in a bin bag in my garden.

Harry (*to Dick*) I keep telling him it's dead.

Tom (*yelling*) I know a dead body's dead, you moron!

Harry Been dead for over twelve months. They keep 'em in this big freezer.

Tom (*grabbing Harry*) I don't want to know, Harry!

Dick (*to Harry*) I've never seen him so aggressive before.

Harry I was just saying that.

Tom (*holding his head*) Ahhhh!

Tom sits in the chair DLC and buries his head in his hands. Dick rests the box on the sofa-bed

Dick We are talking real dead bodies here, yeah?

Harry Well, parts of one.

Tom looks up

Tom (*faintly*) Parts of one?

Harry Well you know what goes on in these teaching hospitals.

Tom (*sarcastically*) No, Harry, my doctor's degree was recently revoked! Why is it only *parts* of a dead body?

Harry Well, the hospital's got all these different departments, hasn't it?

Dick You mean like ear, nose and throat, your heart bloke, your knee bloke ——

Harry Yeah, dentistry, stomach specialist. They've all got to learn on something.

Dick Makes sense.

Harry So they chop up the cadavers so they can go round. Here's your stomach, here's your leg, here's your penis ——

Tom (*yelling*) I get the picture!

Harry After they've all had a go each piece is very nearly wrapped up in a sort of bandage stuff.

Dick Then put in a lucky dip, yeah?

Tom glares at Dick

Harry So, where do you keep your spade and Wellington boots?

Tom looks at Harry maniacally but controlled

Tom Harry, there is only one person who might possibly get buried in my garden ——

Dick Tom, you should give this very serious thought ——

Tom (*glaring at Dick*) I take that back. *Two* people! (*He gets a grip on himself. To Harry*) You get your car round the back, you take that body — those bits of that body — in that bin bag — back to the hospital — right this very second.

Harry No, I can't do that!

Tom (*ominously*) Oh, yes, you can!

Harry No. They think I took it off to be cremated.

Tom (*blankly*) Cremated.

Harry Monday's cadaver day.

Tom (*blankly*) Cadaver —— ?

Dick Ah, like Pancake day, St Valentine's day, Poppy day —— !

Tom Shut up! (*To Harry*) Take it to the crematorium then!

Harry The crematorium thinks it's been delivered already.

Tom (*trying to be calm*) Why would they think that, Harry?

Harry Well, in place of the corpse, I put an old carpet in the body bag and delivered that instead.

Dick (*to Tom*) Doesn't miss a trick, does he?

Harry They cremated it straight away. Never noticed a thing. The ashes have already been sprinkled over Westminster Bridge.

Tom moves to the DL wall and gently bumps his head

Dick (*impressed*) He's a bleedin' genius!

Harry You want to hear the rest of the plan?

Dick You bet!

Tom grabs the box from the sofa-bed

Tom You just take your bloody fags and keep out of this! (*He thrusts the box at Dick*)
Dick But if he's got a good idea ——

Tom pushes Dick up the stairs

Tom (*yelling*) He's *never* had a good idea!

He pushes Dick off

> *Dick exits*

> (*Grabbing Harry by the collar*) You!

He leads Harry to the front door

> Round the back and get rid of that body *now*!
> **Harry** (*stopping*) How, for God's sake?
> **Tom** Dump it somewhere!
> **Harry** You can't just dump a dead body. These things have to be carefully thought through.

Tom opens the front door

Tom I've thought it through! Dump it!

Tom turns Harry to go but Harry turns back

Harry Hang on, before we do anything about the other lot in the garden, why don't we just discuss ——
Tom (*yelling*) Listen, you moronic, bird-brained ... (*He stops*)

Tom closes the door and marches Harry DC

> Other lot? You said, "before we do anything about the other lot in the garden".
> **Harry** Yeah.
> **Tom** (*fearing the worst*) If the other lot's in the garden — (*he points to the garden*) — where's the *other* lot?

Harry Well, most of the bits are out there in the bin bag — and I brought the rest in to show you.

Tom looks blank. Harry points to the four Sainsbury's bags and picks one up. Tom looks mortified and steps to Harry, pointing, horrified. Harry hands him the bag. Tom stares at it for a brief moment

Tom (*yelling*) I don't want it!

He steps back and throws the bag to Harry

  Dick hurries downstairs, heading for the front door

Dick stops on seeing Tom, wide eyed staring at Harry

Dick What's up?
Tom We've got some samples from Sainsbury's!
Dick Samples of what?
Tom Casserole of cadaver!
Dick Casserole of … ?
Harry It's OK. They're all nicely bandaged up.
Tom So no problem then!
Dick Ooo! Let's have a look.

Dick moves to look as:

  Linda enters through the front door carrying a huge bunch of flowers and two Tesco shopping bags

Linda (*entering, calling*) Tom, darling! I'm home …

Tom and Dick immediately sit on the sofa-bed. Harry sits on the arm. Linda puts her two Tesco bags in the chair DLC and then stops on seeing them. They are in their various poses of innocence — Tom is the most strained

  (*Coldly*) Oh, the three musketeers.
Dick (*laughing*) That's what Mum used to call us. The three musty queers.
Linda So that's who you get your sense of humour from. (*To Harry*) Why aren't you at work, Harry?
Harry Just dropped by to say hallo.
Linda (*to Tom*) Haven't you explained we've got Mrs Potter coming at ten?
Tom (*not with it*) Mrs Who?
Linda Mrs *Potter* from the *Agency*.

Tom Oh, that Mrs Agent from the pottery.

Linda (*to Dick*) And I told you to make yourself scarce. Dick.

Dick (*saluting her*) Yes, sir. Just got to carry a few boxes in from the van. There's nothing in 'em, just boxes.

Linda Why do you want them then?

Dick I collect boxes.

Dick exits through the front door

Linda (*referring to the flowers*) I'll stick these in a vase. Don't bother to say goodbye, Harry.

She exits into the kitchen

Tom (*grabbing the four Sainsbury's bags*) Right! You take Sainsbury's finest out of my house *now*!

Tom thrusts them on to Harry and pushes him towards the front door

You get in your car, drive round the back and collect the rest of your bits and pieces.

Behind them, Dick enters struggling with another huge unmarked box and heads for the stairs. This box contains the brandy and is a different shape from the previous box

Harry (*to Tom*) I told you. You can't just dump a dead body!

Tom Take it to that Recycling Centre! Over in Clapham. Now!

Dick I don't know about that. They sometimes have those Inspector blokes up there, don't they?

Tom You piss off! (*To Harry*) You — Clapham!

Harry Look, the plan was to bury the bits and pieces in your back garden, so let's just do that.

Tom There was no plan!

Dick Might be the safest bet now.

Tom Piss off!! (*To Harry*) I'm not having bits of a dead body in my back garden!

Dick Very good for the roses.

Tom raises his fist

I'm pissing off!

Dick hurries upstairs with the box

Harry Tom, why don't you listen to the rest of my plan? It's brilliant.

Tom I've heard enough of your plan. I do not want Alfie Frost to start digging on Monday and have a heart attack in my garden!

Harry Take more than a dead body to give Alfie a heart attack. (*He puts the bags on the sofa-bed*)

Tom And I do not want to be arrested for murder!

Harry No, no, no. I've thought of everything.

Tom You've just uttered the most terrifying words in the English language.

Harry (*picking up one of the Sainsbury's bags*) No-one's going to suspect you, Tom, because we'll bury the bits and pieces —— (*He starts to extricate something from the bag*)

Tom No, don't! (*He covers his eyes*)

Harry — in this old 1940s' army uniform. (*He brings out an old World War II army jacket*)

Tom uncovers his eyes

Dick comes downstairs and, once again, gets intrigued

We'll cut this up in pieces, bury it with all the body parts ——

Dick So when he's dug up the police will think he was murdered by some maniac sixty years ago. (*To Tom*) He is brilliant.

Tom (*heavily sarcastic*) Sixty years ago? Don't you think he would have decomposed by now?!

Dick Over to you, Harry.

Harry We're going to cover the body parts with lemon juice and salt. (*He points in the direction of the other bags*)

Tom Great ! Marinated Cadaver.

Harry It speeds up the deterioration process.

Dick (*in admiration*) I can't believe he's my little brother!

Tom I bloody can.

Harry Lemon juice and salt! It works!

Tom shoves the jacket back in the Sainsbury's bag

I saw it in an episode of *Desperate Housewives*.

Tom Oh well, if it's been on the telly … !

Tom shoves the bag on to Harry

Harry I promise you! The police will think he was killed way back in the 1940s.

Tom Or maybe that I'm a homicidal maniac who likes to bury *Dad's Army* characters in a vinaigrette dressing! (*He delicately picks up another of the Sainsbury's bags. To Harry*) Now take your shopping and go to the dump in Clapham.(*He thrusts the bag at Harry*)

Dick Seriously, Tom, it's bloody ingenious. The publicity will knock a hundred grand off this place.

Tom The Adoption Agency expect my home to be "an environment suitable for the fostering or adoption of an infant" ... (*Yelling*) Not the cellar of Sweeney Todd's bloody barber shop! (*Picking up the other two bags*) Now, for the last time —— !

Linda enters from the kitchen with the flowers in a vase

Linda (*entering*) Here we are ... !

The three of them quickly sit on the sofa-bed and then go into their various innocent modes. Linda looks at them. Tom is still clutching two of the Sainsbury bags

Tom For the last time — I want to say thank you. Thank you, Harry. Thank you, Dick, for your good wishes and we'll certainly consider naming the baby after you.

Linda We bloody won't! (*She puts the flowers on the table*)

Tom Not if it's a girl, I've explained that, haven't I?

Linda lifts Harry up by his collar and marches him to the front door

Linda Thanks for calling, Harry! We'll let you know how we get on with the baby.

Tom (*rushing up with the two Sainsbury's bags*) Hang on, he can't go yet!

Linda Wrong!

She pushes Harry out and slams the door

Harry exits

I got cakes and biscuits for Mrs Potter. Thanks.

She takes the two Sainsbury's bags from Tom and heads for the kitchen. For a moment Tom and Dick are shell-shocked. They then look at each other, horrified, and back to Linda

Tom
Dick } (*yelling together*) No!! (*They rise*)

Linda (*jumping*) Bloody hell!

Tom starts to walk slowly towards her with false calm

Tom Those — are my bags.
Linda (*bemused*) What?
Tom They're my bags — and I want them. (*He takes hold of the bags and tries — ever so gently — to pull them towards him*)
Linda Don't be daft. (*She roughly pulls the bags back*)
Tom My bags. (*He gently pulls them to him*)
Linda They're my bags, actually. (*She roughly pulls them to her*)
Dick (*taking a pace in*) I don't think the to-ing and fro-ing of the ——
Linda You shut up!
Dick (*stepping back*) Of course. (*He sits on the sofa-bed*)
Linda (*to Tom*) I don't know what the hell's the matter with you! I've just bought this lot at Tesco's for Mrs Potter.
Tom (*faintly*) Sainsbury's.
Linda What?
Tom Sainsbury's.

He gently pulls the bags back and points to the Tesco bags on the chair. She looks at them

  (*Pointing*) Those yours. Tesco's. These mine. Sainsbury's.
Linda When did you go to Sainsbury's? You haven't left the house.

Tom opens his mouth — nothing comes out

Dick (*rising*) They delivered.
Tom They delivered.
Linda Sainsbury's don't deliver.

Tom looks to Dick

Dick You have to ask them very nicely.
Linda (*to Tom*) What did you get then? (*She roughly pulls the bags back*)
Tom (*shrugging*) Just a few bits and pieces.
Dick Oh my God! (*He closes his eyes and sits again*)

Tom realizes what he's said

Tom It's a surprise — from Sainsbury's — for Mrs Potter. (*He gently pulls the bags to him*)

Linda Mrs Potter?
Tom Well, I thought *you'd* got her the flowers the least I could do was give her — what's in here.
Linda Which is?! (*She roughly pulls the bags back*)
Tom A surprise. (*He gently pulls them to him*)
Linda Look, this interview has got to go perfect. I don't want any surprises. Now what did you get her?

She pulls both of the bags out of Tom's hands and goes to look inside

Tom } (*yelling together*) No!!
Dick
Linda (*jumping*) God almighty.
Dick Linda, love. It's Mrs Potter's surprise. If you get the surprise where's the surprise for Mrs Potter?
Linda If you don't shut up I'll kick you very hard where it hurts most.
Dick Point taken.
Linda (*going to open the bag*) Now let's see ——— !
Tom } (*yelling together*) { No, don't please ——— !
Dick   { Linda — !

But she already has. Her face is blank

Linda What the hell's this?
Tom I can explain, sweetheart!
Linda These are a present for Mrs Potter?
Dick Well, it's not easy when you don't know somebody very well.
Linda (*pressing on*) You're going to give Mrs Potter a load of *lemons*?

She takes a lemon out of the bag. Tom and Dick stare for a moment and then laugh foolishly

Tom Yeah!
Dick Yeah!
Tom It was Dick's idea.

Dick stops laughing

Dick Well, it was Harry's idea, actually.
Linda (*flatly*) To give her a bunch of lemons.
Dick } (*together*) Yeah! (*They laugh again more foolishly*)
Tom
Linda Why?

They stop laughing. Tom looks at Dick

Dick The idea was to make — lemonade.
Tom Lemonade.
Dick For Mrs Potter. And present it to her as a gift.
Tom (*to Linda*) Gift.
Linda Lemonade?
Dick Old Kerwood family tradition. (*To Tom*) Harry reminded us, didn't he?
Tom Yeah! Harry reminded us. Don't know who started it. Granddad?
Dick Granddad. Great Granddad.
Linda (*taking out a large packet from the bag*) And the salt?
Tom Yeah. That's what gives it the body.
Dick (*quickly*) The kick!
Tom The kick!!
Dick Wow! Hits you right there.

Tom quickly picks up the Tesco bags

Tom (*to Linda*) Here's your Tesco bags, sweetheart.

He thrusts the two Tesco bags at her and grabs the two Sainsbury's bags

Linda (*to Dick*) Listen, before you make your stupid lemonade will you
    finish getting those damn boxes of yours out of Tom's van. Then clear off!
Dick (*saluting*) Yes, ma'am.
Linda (*referring to her bags, to Tom*) I'll unpack this lot. And we'll give Mrs
    Potter coffee in the dining-room. Looks smarter. (*She opens the kitchen
    door*)

*Harry is leaning against the kitchen door listening. He is clutching a
heavily stuffed, heavy duty black bin liner bag, tied at the top. As the door
opens he falls in and he and the bin bag fall over the chair DLC and hit the
floor with Harry's face buried in the bin bag*

Tom and Dick are mortified

Harry (*brightly*) Hi, there.
Linda What the hell were you doing in my kitchen?
Harry Coming through. Hi, Tom! Hi, Dick!

Tom and Dick are staring at him and the bag blankly

Linda (*pointing to the stuffed bin bag*) And what the hell's in there?

Harry (*shrugging*) Just something I brought for Tom.

She looks at Tom. Tom, mesmerized, nods

Linda (*to Harry*) What is it, oranges?
Harry Oranges?
Linda To go with the bloody lemons.
Harry Lemons?
Linda (*pointing at the bin bag*) Your granddad!
Harry Granddad? (*He looks at the bin bag and back to Linda*)

She storms into the kitchen

There is a pause and then Tom suddenly busts out of his mesmerized state

Tom (*to Harry, a maniacal outburst*) What in God's name do you think you're doing?! Why the hell are you bringing that lot in here?! Have you totally lost it, Harry?!
Dick Knowing Harry he'd prefer one question at a time.
Tom Shut up! (*To Harry*) What are those nut cutlets doing in our living-room?!
Harry Safest bet.
Tom Safest bet?
Harry Yeah. I drove the car round the back like you suggested ——
Tom (*impatiently*) Yeah, yeah!
Harry — and I was going to come through and get my two other Sainsbury bags from you ——
Tom (*impatiently*) Yeah, yeah!
Harry — to put in the bin bag with their counterparts ——
Dick Could we just skip to episode six please?
Harry Well, in the garden I encountered a problem.
Tom (*impatiently*) What bloody problem?
Harry Alfie Frost is out there measuring up for your conservatory.
Tom (*looking towards the window*) Eh?
Harry He was sitting on my bin bag smoking a fag.
Dick Here, he might like to buy a few cartons of my cigarettes——
Tom (*interrupting*) Shut up!
Harry I thought it safer to bring it in here in case Alfie suddenly found himself sitting on an upturned finger of one of the ——
Tom (*interrupting, yelling*) Harry! (*He puts his two Sainsbury bags beside the bin bag. Struggling to untie the top of the bin bag; crazily*) Forget Alfie bloody Frost! You are going to the dump in Clapham with this lot and keeping out of my sight for at least six months! (*To Dick*) And you are getting your fags and brandy up to your flat. The flat which I'm giving you notice to quit as of now!

Dick ⎫ (*together*) I've never seen him so aggressive before.
Harry ⎭
Tom (*to Harry, yelling*) Piss — (*to Dick*) off!
Dick We won't bother with the lemonade then.

Tom turns, eyes ablaze

Dick hurries out through the front door

Tom returns to the knot which is now undone

Tom And if you ever get another brilliant idea, Harry — ! (*He opens the top of the bin bag — the smell hits him*) Cor! What a pong!

He quickly holds the top of the bin bag closed as Harry opens the window

Harry! That is not nice! (*He opens the top again and shoves the two Sainsbury bags in during the following*)
Harry I reckon it must have got a bit hot in the boot of my car.
Tom I'll give you a bit hot!

Linda appears in the kitchen doorway. She now wears an apron and is carrying a bottle of tomato ketchup

The Sainsbury bags are now in the bin bag but Tom hasn't had time to tie the top

Linda (*entering, calling*) Tom ... !

Tom and Harry quickly sit on the bin bag and look innocent

Now, what're you playing at?
Tom Just having a little chat with Harry.
Linda Well, your Mr Frost says is it OK to start on Tuesday rather than Monday?
Tom Tuesday. No problem.
Linda (*moving to them*) And Harry, I want you out of here before Mrs Potter ... (*She stops*) What's that smell?
Tom Smell?
Linda It suddenly hit me.
Tom (*sniffing*) Oh, yeah. You mean that sweet smell.
Linda Sweet ... ?! It'll be that bloody bin bag of Harry's.
Tom No!
Linda Something's gone off in there.

Tom No!
Linda Let's have a look! (*She goes to pull the bin bag from under Tom and Harry*)
Tom ⎱ (*together*) No!
Harry ⎰

Tom jumps up and quickly pushes her to below the sofa-bed

Tom Don't make a scene!
Linda What?
Tom Don't make a scene, it was Harry.
Linda What was?
Tom That pong! (*Pointing*) It was Harry.
Linda (*surprised*) That smell was ——— ?
Tom Yeah!
Harry Now, wait a minute ——— !
Tom (*quickly*) There's no need to be embarrassed, Harry!
Harry Eh?
Tom (*to Linda*) That's what we were chatting about. He can't help it. Poor boy's developed this nervous stomach thing. (*He blows a raspberry*) It just comes on suddenly. (*He blows another raspberry*) No apparent reason. (*He blows two quick raspberries. Then stops*) The doctor says it's an intermittent (*another raspberry*) fault.

An agitated Dick rushes in from the front door, slamming it behind him

Dick (*entering*) Tom, you'd better come and … ! (*He sees Linda. Cheerfully*) Hi, Linda.
Linda (*tersely*) Have you moved those boxes yet?
Dick Coming along.
Linda Well, be quick about it. (*To Tom*) I'll tell Mr Frost he can start Tuesday. (*Tersely*) And, Harry, I'm very sorry about your condition ———

She pulls Harry off the bin bag and, again reacts to the smell

——— but I don't want that smell around when Mrs Potter's here. Now you get back to the hospital. And while you're there see one of those gastro specialists.

She storms back into the kitchen, slamming the door shut

Tom immediately rushes to the bin bag and ties the top

Dick Tom, we've got a slight ——— !

Tom Shut up!

Harry (*interrupting*) Tom, that was not a nice thing to say.

Dick (*to Harry*) Shut up. (*To Tom*) We've got a problem.

Tom First bloody things first. (*To Harry*) You and your cadaver to Clapham!

He pushes Harry to the bin bag

Dick I have to tell you something.

Tom Shut up.

Harry I can't drag that through the kitchen with Linda there.

Tom I know that. You're going through the window.

Harry Hang on, it's heavier now. More bits and pieces. The car's parked in the back street at the far end of the garden.

During the following, Tom sits Harry on the window sill

Tom (*in one breath*) OK! Go and grab the wheelbarrow, bring the barrow to the window, shove that lot in the barrow, wheel the barrow down the garden to the back gate, put the bin bag in your car and piss off to Clapham.

Dick (*to Tom*) Will you listen for God's sake?!

Tom No, I've done with listening!

Tom pushes Harry who falls backwards into the garden

Harry (*as he goes*) Ahhhh!

Harry exits

There is a loud crash as Harry falls into galvanized dustbins

Tom (*to Dick*) Right. I'm in charge now.

Dick That's good, because you've got visitors out there. (*He points to the front door*)

Tom (*worried*) Not Mrs Potter?

Dick No, I've been trying to tell you! I went to take one of the boxes out of the van ——

Tom Yeah! Yeah!

Dick — and in amongst the cigarettes and brandy ——

Tom Yeah! Yeah!

Dick (*flatly*) — you've got two illegal immigrants in the back of your van.

Tom's face goes blank. He then turns round, walks slowly to the stairs and leans on the newel post. He then returns to Dick

Tom Two illegal immigrants?
Dick They must have sneaked in while I was in that café in Calais. An old boy and some young fellah.

Tom is unable to speak

They won't get out. They're scared shitless. They must be looking for asylum.
Tom They've bloody found one!

Tom collapses into the armchair DLC. *Dick hands Tom a tatty piece of paper*

Dick The old boy gave me this. It's an address and telephone number — in Shepherd's Bush.

Tom, dazed, looks down at it

Tom It's in a foreign language.

Dick turns the piece of paper the right way up. Tom stares at it

Harry appears at the window

Harry I can't find the wheelbarrow!

Tom slowly looks up

Tom This was going to be the happiest day of my life.
Dick (*encouragingly*) You'll sort it out, mate.

Tom rises and turns on him

Tom (*with fake amazement*) Oh, *I'll* sort it out, will I? I'll sort out your fags and your immigrants and his chopped liver and bacon, yeah? No! *You* will sort this out! You will ring the police right now. (*He picks up the cordless phone*)
Harry What's happened?
Tom I'll tell you what's happened, Mr Genius of the morgue. Your fellow genius of the fags here has lumbered us with two illegal immigrants.
Dick (*to Harry*) Must have sneaked on in Calais.
Harry (*delighted*) Great. They can give us a hand with the body.
Tom No, they bloody can't!
Harry They'll be bloody cheap!

Tom (*giving Harry a steely glare*) They are illegal immigrants. They will be handed over (*to Dick*) to the proper authorities!

Dick What about me and the van load of cigarettes?

Tom You'll get a small fine, that's all.

Dick It'll be more than that. I'm still on probation from the last job.

Tom Probation?

Dick I could have sworn I told you.

Tom No, you didn't bloody tell me!

Dick (*to Harry*) I told *you*, didn't I, Harry?

Harry Yeah, he told me.

Tom (*to Harry*) Shut up!

Dick I was stitched up, mind you.

Tom (*ominously*) What for?

Dick Illegally smuggling 400,000 cigarettes.

Tom So you'll get a bloody big fine. Now ring the police! (*He holds out the telephone*)

Dick There's something else.

Tom (*flatly*) What?

Dick Well, I shouldn't have been driving the van in the first place.

Tom (*flatly*) Why not?

Dick I haven't got a driving licence.

Tom You haven't got a … ?!

Dick (*to Harry*) I told you, didn't I.

Harry Yeah, he told me.

Tom (*to Harry*) Shut up!!

Dick I was stitched up, Tom. It's not right them banning me for seven years.

Tom Seven years?!

Dick It was way over the top.

Tom What the hell had you done?

Dick I thought I told you.

Tom No, you didn't bloody tell me!

Dick (*to Harry*) I told *you*, didn't I?

Harry Yeah, he told me.

Tom (*to Harry*) Shut up!!!

Dick I promise you, Tom, the machine was all to cock. It went red before I'd even breathed into the bloody thing.

Tom (*staggered*) You were had for drunk driving?!

Harry He's been more pissed than that and got home.

Tom (*to Harry*) Shut up! (*To Dick*) Ring the police!

Dick The country's stuffed with refugees. Are two more going to make any difference?

Tom These are *illegal immigrants*.

Harry We-ell — half the blokes have got a legit piece of paper, half haven't.

Tom (*to Harry*) Will you shut up!!!! (*To Dick*) The police!

Dick Tom, I've got a plan.

Tom I don't want any more bloody plans.

Dick The police is not the best option — considering your position.

Tom Ring the pol — ! (*He stops*) How do you mean, "my position"?

Dick Well, I was driving your van, wasn't I. They'll confiscate it, slap a hefty fine on you and ask questions afterwards. And it's not the best time to have the place crawling with police, is it? I mean Linda will have to be told, your adoption lady's coming, you still haven't sorted out that cadaver.

There is a momentary pause

Tom OK ... What's the plan? (*He bangs the phone down*)

Dick Good lad. Now we ring that number in Shepherd's Bush and explain we've got their two illegals here. Come and collect them right away. Then, when they get here we'll say how about a small commission, please.

Tom I don't want a small commission!

Harry Quite right, ask for a big one.

Tom You just keep out of this.

Dick I'll nip upstairs and get my mobile. (*He moves to the stairs*)

Tom (*urgently*) Don't waste time! Use that. (*He points to the phone*)

Dick Not wise. A call from your phone is traceable.

Tom Well, they can trace a call from your mobile, can't they?

Dick Who cares? I nicked it from a bloke in that café in Calais.

Dick hurries upstairs

During the following, Tom backs Harry to the window and sits him

Tom (*to Harry*) Will you get the wheelbarrow?!

Harry I told you, I can't find the wheelbarrow.

Tom Did you look in the shed?

Harry No.

Tom Well, look, you idiot!

The kitchen door opens and Linda appears. She is carrying a folded tablecloth, plates and cutlery on a tray

Linda (*entering, calling*) Tom!

Tom neatly pushes Harry backwards off the window ledge into the garden (no crash this time) and leans on the window ledge

Harry exits

Harry (*as he disappears*) Ahhh!

Linda turns on hearing the noise

Tom Ahhh! — Ahhh! — Ahhh! what a lovely view! Do you know I've never noticed it before. The way the back wall, the telegraph pole and the garden shed give a feeling of ——
Linda (*interrupting*) I've never seen you in such a state!
Tom Well, I'm nervous, aren't I! First time I've adopted a body — (*quickly*) a baby!
Linda (*seeing the bin bag*) And why is that still in the living-room? (*She kicks it*)
Tom Don't — do that please! I mean show a little respect for the rubbish.
Linda I thought it was something Harry was giving you.
Tom Yeah, that's right, it is.
Linda (*surprised*) Harry brought you over his rubbish to give you?
Tom Well, no, that'd be stupid, wouldn't it? It's his rubbishy old clothes. You know, stuff he hasn't worn for years. Thought it might suit me.
Linda You've got a wardrobe full of stuff you never wear.
Tom You're right. We'll give 'em to Oxfam.
Linda Never mind Oxfam. Get it out of here before Mrs Potter arrives!
Tom Definitely.
Linda And take these into the dining-room while I finish the sandwiches. (*She hands the tray to Tom*)
Tom Definitely.

He turns her to go back into the kitchen

Linda (*turning back*) Have those two layabout brothers of yours gone yet?
Tom Oh, yeah, and not coming back.

Without thinking, Tom hands her the tray and turns her as:

Dick hurtles on to the landing

Dick Tom — ! (*Seeing Linda; politely*) Sorry, wrong room.

Dick hurries back upstairs

Linda If he puts in an appearance while Mrs Potter's here he'll end up the highest soprano in Kennington.

She exits into the kitchen with the tray, shutting the door

Dick's head appears upstairs, he quickly checks that Linda has gone

Dick Tom — !
Tom Have you got your mobile?!
Dick Never mind that, you got a copper checking your van!
Tom What?!
Dick He's writing down the details of your tax disc.
Tom Bloody hell!

Tom hesitates, then opens the front door a fraction to peer out — the door bursts wide open

Katerina rushes in pulling a terrified, puffing and panting Andreas behind her. Katerina is a Kosovan in her late twenties/early thirties, a poorly dressed peasant, buxom and attractive and wearing a cap. She is confident and dangerous. She carries a packed holdall on her back and a long bladed knife in her hand. Andreas is a small eighty-year-old shabby Kosovan, stooped and weather-beaten, wearing a long scarf around his waist and on his back a very old haversack. Katerina pulls Andreas across her, slams the front door and leans against it. NB: Katerina and Andreas speak Albanian. In the script is first printed the phonetical Albanian, then [English translation] followed by the actual Albanian

Katerina Politzei! Politzei!
Andreas (*terrified, pointing*) Politzei! Politzei!

There is a brief pause

Tom (*in bemused amazement*) What the bloody hell's going on?
Dick I dunno but the good news is she's not a fellah is she?
Katerina Politzei. Poh narn dee-ek! [Police. Coming after us!] POLITZEI. PO NA NDJEK!
Dick At a rough guess I reckon that copper's after them.
Andreas Politzei! Politzei! Kor tay fsheehem?! [I'll hide in here?!] KU TE FSHIHEM?!

Andreas opens the bedroom door and runs in slamming the door

Tom Hey, come back, you cheeky bugger!

As Tom goes to chase Andreas the doorbell goes. They freeze

Dick It'll be that copper!

Tom Quick, before Linda comes in. Take her up to your bedroom!
Dick Gets better all the time!

Dick takes Katerina upstairs

Tom hurries to the bin liner

Tom God! (*He dithers for a moment then he rushes to the window and leans out. Calling urgently*) Harry! Harry!

The doorbell goes again

God! (*He straightens up and bangs his head on the window*) Ahh! (*He quickly drags the bin bag to the window and with a huge effort lifts it*)

Linda opens the kitchen door — not seeing Tom by the window

Linda (*calling urgently*) Tom — !
Tom Ooo!

Tom turns and sits on the window ledge with the bin bag in his lap. Linda looks at him

Linda What are you doing now?
Tom Getting rid of Harry's old clothes. (*He turns and lets the bin bag fall out through the window*) There we are. Dead easy. Drop 'em off at Oxfam tomorrow. Back you go into the kitchen.
Linda Was that Mrs Potter at the door?
Tom At the door?
Linda The front doorbell went just now!
Tom I didn't hear it.

He turns her towards the kitchen as the doorbell goes again. She turns back

I did then.

Linda pushes him towards the front door

Linda She's twenty minutes early. Let her in while I tidy myself up, in the bedroom.
Tom Good idea!

She heads towards the bedroom. Tom suddenly realizes that Andreas is in the bedroom

Tom (*yelling*) No!!!
Linda (*jumping*) God!

He pulls her across him pushing her to the kitchen

Tom Finish the sandwiches first. I'll look after Mrs Potter.
Linda Good thinking. Take her into the dining-room. Give me five minutes.

The doorbell goes again

Tom Take ten. You've got to tidy yourself up. You look a right mess.

He pushes her into the kitchen and slams the door

   Linda exits

He starts to move away then hurriedly returns and locks the kitchen door

   Rule three, lock door with key.

The front doorbell goes again — insistently. He quickly tiptoes towards the front door and peeps through the letter-box

   Andreas appears around the bedroom door

Andreas Hey!
Tom (*jumping*) Ahh! (*Catching his fingers in the letter-box*) Oooo!
Andreas Ar yemee tay seagoat por te darlim kay kettay? [Hey! Is it safe to come out?] A JEMI TE SIGURT POITE DALIM QE KETEJ?
Tom (*going to him*) Me no speaky Chinese, you stay in there!

Andreas moves to the phone, lifts the receiver and gives it to Tom

Andreas Telefono! Tee telefono. Sheepherd's Bowsh tee. Tee. Sheepherd's Bowsh. Telfono! Alo, alo! Sheepherd's Bowsh. [Telephone! You telephone. Shepherd's Bush you. You. Shepherd's Bush. Telephone! Hallo, hallo! Sheepherd's Bowsh?] TELEFONO! TI TELEFONO! SHEEPHERD'S BOWSH TI. TI. SHEEPHERD'S BOWSH TELEFONO. ALO, ALO! SHEEPHERDS BOWSH!
Tom Goodbye, goodbye Sheepherd's Bowsh!
Andreas Ello, ello.
Tom Goodbye goodbye.

He pushes Andreas into the bedroom

Andreas exits

Rule three, lock door with key.

He locks the bedroom door and hurries to the front door. He takes a deep breath and opens it

Constable Downs steps in. He is a homely police officer in his mid-forties. At the moment he is very agitated

Tom Oh! Good-morning, Officer.
Downs Are you all right, sir?
Tom Fine, fine, never better. Why, is something wrong?

Downs moves down into the room, looking around

Downs Well, you took a bit of time to open the door and I thought maybe those two people had ... have two persons just rushed through into your house?
Tom (*innocently*) Two persons?
Downs Look, I'd stopped to check that van outside your house ——
Tom My van, yes.
Downs The rear doors were wide open ——
Tom Thanks for telling me. I'll deal with it. (*He indicates for Downs to go*)
Downs (*pressing on*) — and inside the van were a large quantity of boxes.
Tom Boxes, yes. My boxes.
Downs Well, as the vehicle was unattended I decided to take down the particulars of the van.
Tom Very wise. (*He indicates for Downs to go*)
Downs While I was engaged in that activity at the front of the van I saw two persons — a young lady and a rather elderly gentleman — leap from the rear of the van and run through your front door.
Tom (*nodding*) A young — er — and an elderly — er — yes, my wife and Uncle Bert.
Downs (*surprised*) Your wife?
Tom Yes. And dear old Uncle Bert. They're staying with us. (*Quickly*) Well, my wife *lives* here, of course! Uncle Bert's having a little break. Well, it's more serious than that really. He's walked out on my Auntie Flo. After fifty years. He just turned round and said, "It's over, Flo".

He turns Downs to go but Downs turns back

Downs Yes, but what exactly were your wife and Uncle — er ——

Tom Bert. I know what you're going to ask! What were my wife and Uncle Bert doing in the back of my van.

Downs I was actually, yes.

Tom Looking for our cat. She's always disappearing. Worries my wife no end. She'd be lost without her pussy. It's all right though. She was up a tree flirting with that Tom next door. The cat, not my wife. Is there anything else, Constable? It's rather a hectic morning round here.

Downs (*grudgingly*) I suppose not. But, if I were you, sir, I'd go and lock that van of yours.

Tom Definitely. Thanks for everything, Constable.

He turns Downs to go as the kitchen door handle is rattled followed by banging on the door. Downs turns back. Tom smiles

Linda (*off*) Hey! Tom!

Downs looks to Tom. Tom crosses to the kitchen door

Tom (*shouting*) Get on with the sandwiches! (*To Downs*) If I don't lock her in she gets nothing done. (*He smiles at Downs*)

Downs looks at him blankly and goes out through the front door

Tom shuts the door

(*Collapsing*) Oh, my God!

Dick appears on the landing

Dick Your wife and Uncle Bert — *brilliant*!

Linda bangs on the kitchen door

Linda (*off*) Tom! This door won't open!

Tom (*calling*) It's stuck! I'm looking for something to force it open!

Dick Bloody brilliant.

Andreas bangs on the bedroom door

Andreas (*off*) Happay cutter dare. [Open this door.] HAPE KETE DARE.

Tom Shut up!

Dick (*taking the mobile phone from his pocket*) Here's the mobile. Where's the Shepherd's Bush number?

Tom First things first. Take that old bloke upstairs before Linda sees him!

Dick He's that girl's granddad by the way. It's amazing what you can pick up with the old sign language, you know. They've had a dreadful time! Terrible! The whole family! (*He puts his mobile away and during the following does a convoluted quick set of mimes*) She was telling me, you see. The (*pointing to the bedroom*) "old boy's" "daughter" who is the "mother" of the "young lady" up (*pointing*) there — which makes him (*pointing*) her (*pointing*) "granddad" — her (*pointing*) "mummy" — escaped from Kosova with "two" other "daughters" — her "husband" was "brutally killed" — not *her* (*pointing upstairs*) "husband" — her (*pointing*) "mummy's" "husband" — the "old boy's" "daughter's" "husband" — her (*pointing*) "daddy" — Now "granddad" and "her up there" (*pointing*) have "escaped" Kosova, too. "Terrible journey" — "eight" days. Now "today" — thanks to "us" — they "join" "Mummy" and "two" "daughters" in United Kingdom.

Tom looks at him blankly

Tom (*calmly*) I think I might have missed some of that.

Dick (*starting to mime again*) "The old boy" and the girl up ——

Tom (*interrupting*) Shut up!

Andreas (*off, banging on the bedroom door*) Happay cutter dare. [Open this door.] HAPE KETE DARE.

Tom Shut up!

Dick You have to do it in sign language.

Tom (*to Dick, miming as he speaks*) Shut up!

Tom moves to the bedroom door. There is more banging on the kitchen door

Linda (*off, from the kitchen*) What the hell's going on in there?

Tom Won't be a moment. I'm — er …

Dick Looking for the hammer.

Tom (*calling*) Looking for the hammer!

Dick Brilliant!

Andreas (*off, banging on the door*) Happay cutter dare. [Open this door.] HAPE KETE DARE.

Tom opens the bedroom door

Tom Come on, you!

He pulls Andreas out and across him and shuts the bedroom door

Andreas Koo ershta viser eemay? [Where is my granddaughter?] KU
ESHTE VAJZA IME?
Tom Very likely. Come on.

He goes to push Andreas towards the stairs but Andreas stops

Andreas Eeyo! Chvar po ee baynee visus seemay? [No! What have you done
with my granddaughter?] JO! GFARE PO I BENI VAJZES SIME?
Tom And the same to you!

He goes to push him but an angry Andreas turns on him

Andreas Viser eemer! Kor ershter viser eemer?! [My granddaughter!
Where is my granddaughter?!] VAJZES SIME! KU ESHTE VAJZA
IME?!
Tom Shut up! My wife is in the kitchen.
Andreas Viser eemer! Kor ershter viser eemer?! [My granddaughter!
Where is my granddaughter?!] VAJZES SIE! KU ESHTE VAJZA IME?!
Tom Shut up!
Dick (*quickly*) Hold it. Leave it to the interpreter. (*To Andreas, slowly
miming*) Are *you* "asking" after the "whereabouts" of *your* pretty "grand-
daughter"?

Andreas looks blank for a moment

Andreas (*brightly*) Yais! Yais! [Yes! Yes!] (*Miming*) Mee viser coo ershta?
[My granddaughter where is she?] JAIS! JAIS! MAE VAJZA KU
ESHTE?
Tom Bloody hell!
Dick Patience, Thomas. Think what he's been through. (*To Andreas,
miming*) Your pretty granddaughter is upstairs (*pointing*) with me (*point-
ing*).
Andreas Nook po kooptoy. [I don't understand.] NUK PO KUPTOJ.
Dick (*emphasizing, miming*) Your pretty "granddaughter" *upstairs* with *me*
in *bedroom*.
Andreas (*suddenly suspicious, emphasizing the mime*) Viser eemer lart.
[My granddaughter upstairs.] VAJZA IME LART. (*Pointing*) Met oo.
[With you.] ME TY.
Dick He's got it! (*Pointing*) *She — me — bedroom.*
Andreas (*furiously*) Tee perbindush. [You swine.] TY PERBINDESH.
(*Pointing*) Viser eemer lart. [My granddaughter upstairs.] VAJZA IME
LART. (*Pointing*) Met oo. [With you.] ME TY. (*He mimes a quick pelvis
thrust*)
Dick No, no, no, no, no! *Me* no your pretty granddaughter ... (*He mimes a
quick pelvis thrust*)

Andreas Perbindush! Perbindush! [Swine! Swine!] PERBINDESH!
PERBINDESH!

Yelling he starts to throttle Dick and drags him over the sofa-bed

Tom Shut up!

*Andreas has Dick on the sofa-bed by the collar and is bouncing him up and
down*

Dick Help!
Tom (*calling into the kitchen*) I'll turn the radio down. (*To Andreas*) Pack
it in.
Linda (*off*) Tom!

The kitchen door handle rattles. More knocking

Tom (*calling*) I've nearly found the hammer!

Katerina hurries downstairs to see Andreas throttling Dick

Katerina Jushi, jushi, chvar pon doth uttoo? [Granddad, Granddad, what is
happening down here?] GFARE PO NDODH KETU?
Dick There's been a bit of a misunderstanding.

Andreas throws Dick aside and hurries to her

Amdreas Katerina! Ay vogler eemay! Kie perbindush — [Katerina! My
little baby! Did that swine —] KATERINA! E VOGLA IME! KY
PERBINDESH — (*He points to Dick then does a quick pelvis thrust*)
Katerina Eyo! Eyo! [No! No!] YO! YO!
Dick (*to Katerina*) Tell him, "me nice man".
Katerina (*pointing to Dick*) Aye ershter nyeree shome im airy! [He is a very
nice man.] AI ESHTE NJERI SHUME I MIRE!
Andreas (*pointing to Dick*) Aye ershter im airy. [He is a nice man?] AI
ESHTE I MIRE?
Katerina Po shoom im airy. [Yes, very nice.] PO SHUME I MIRE.
Andreas (*hurrying to Dick*) May vee-en kaych! May vee-en kaych! [I'm so
sorry! I'm so sorry!] ME VJEN KEQ! ME VJEN KEQ!

He smothers Dick in kisses

Dick It's all right, it's all right!

Andreas (*kissing Tom*) May vee-en kaych! May vee-en kaych! [I'm so sorry! I'm so sorry!] ME VJEN KEQ! ME VJEN KEQ!
Tom It's all right!!

There is a banging on the kitchen door. They all freeze

Linda (*off*) Open this bloody door!
Tom I'll have to get Linda out of the house while we deal with this lot.
Dick Bloody hell!
Tom (*to Dick*) Get these two upstairs!
Dick What about ringing Shepherd's Bush?
Tom In a minute! Just keep 'em out of the bloody way while I deal with Linda.
Dick (*to Andreas*) Come on! (*Miming*) Upstairs.
Tom Just bloody push 'em off.
Dick Come on, Granddad.

Dick pushes them upstairs

Andreas May vee-en kaych! May vee-en kaych! [I'm so sorry! I'm so sorry!] ME VJEN KEQ! ME VJEN KEQ!

He kisses Dick and won't stop

Dick Why don't you let your granddaughter apologize for you?

Dick, Andreas and Katerina exit

Tom (*yelling upstairs*) Keep 'em quiet!

There is banging on the kitchen door

Linda (*off*) I'm going to kick this bloody door in!

Tom quickly unlocks the door and opens it

A furious Linda barges in with her foot raised

Tom (*sweetly*) Sorry about the delay, darling.

He pulls Linda across him and closes the door

Linda I thought the door was stuck.

Tom No it was locked.

Linda (*snatching the key from him*) Why the hell didn't you check that in the first place?

Tom I was too busy looking for the hammer.

Linda Silly bugger! Well, was it Mrs Potter at the door?

Tom Er — no! (*Brightly*) It was her secretary.

Linda (*surprised*) Her secretary?

Tom Yes. She didn't stay long. Very apologetic. Change of plan. The meeting's at the Agency.

Linda (*bewildered*) The Agency?

During the following, he gets Linda's coat and makes three abortive attempts to put it on her: inside out, back to front then on himself

Tom Apparently there's been a huge influx of orphans from the Far East. Mrs Potter has to arrange all the adoptions. She's up to her eyes. Could *we* go *there*. Well, could *you* go in the first place. That's what Mrs Potter does. So the secretary was telling me. First the prospective mother then the prospective father. Makes sense.

Linda Why the hell didn't they tell us earlier?

Tom Well, if you've suddenly got five hundred orphans on your hands. She's expecting you at ten o'clock. I'm due at eleven. You'll have to hurry. You know where the Agency is. Grab a taxi on the corner.

Linda God, I feel sick!

Tom Nice taxi ride, do you good.

Linda But I've made the coffee. There's cakes and sandwiches.

Tom We'll save them for the baby. 'Bye, sweetheart. Kiss Mrs Potter for me.

Linda You're crazy but I love you!

Tom So do I!

He pushes her out the front door

Linda exits

(*Singing to her as she goes*) We're adopting a bubby-doo! We're adopting a bubby-doo! We're adopting a ... (*He closes the door. Speaking*) Bloody hell!

Dick appears on the stairs

Dick *Five hundred orphans*, you deserve a medal!

Tom Shut up and get down here!

Harry appears at the window

Harry Tom! Is it all clear now?

Tom Yeah, until Linda comes storming back from the Agency.

Harry Agency? (*He climbs in*)

Dick (*to Harry*) I tell you. Big brother surpassed himself. (*Miming*) He told her there'd been a big influx of orphans from the Far East and she had to ——

Tom Shut up. Give me your mobile so I can get those two immigrants out of your flat.

Tom grabs the mobile from Dick

Harry What the hell are they doing up there?

Tom (*sarcastically*) I invited them in for coffee, didn't I?

Harry That was a very nice gesture, Tom.

Tom Shut up!

Dick The old boy's a hoot and the pretty granddaughter is a corker.

Harry Can't wait!

Tom Oy! Did you find the wheelbarrow?

Harry (*indicating the window*) The carriage awaits.

Tom Just get that bin bag into your car before Mrs Potter arrives, and piss off to Clapham.

Harry OK. Where is it?

Tom What, your car?

Harry No, the bin bag.

Tom The bin bag is outside the window, Harry!

Harry No it's not.

Tom I just dropped it there!

Harry Not there now.

Tom hesitates, thrusts the mobile on to Dick and then rushes to look out of the window. He turns back and grabs Harry

Tom What have you done with that cadaver, Harry?

Harry Nothing, honest. I went down to the shed, got the wheelbarrow, came back, had a bit of a chat with Alfie … (*He stops*) Alfie Frost!

Tom (*bemused*) Alfie Frost?

Dick (*helpfully*) That's your builder.

Tom I know that! (*To Harry*) What about him?

Harry (*appalled*) He's just about to leave!

Tom (*concerned*) What's that got to do with your cadaver?

Harry He's taking our bin bag to the Oxfam shop in the High Street.

Tom looks blank for a moment then sinks into the chair and buries his head in his hands

(*To Dick*) I didn't realize it was the one with the body parts. I thought they were still in here on the floor. (*To Tom who still has his head buried*) Apparently Linda saw Alfie packing up and asked him to drop off the bin bag at Oxfam.

Dick Some idiot must have told Linda it was old clothes in there.

Tom slowly looks up

Tom You're right, it was *this* idiot! Because *this* idiot comes from a *family* of bloody idiots!

He grabs Harry and pushes him to the front door

Get in your car now and you get to that Oxfam shop before Alfie does and you get that bloody bin bag back off him!

Dick Hold it, Tom. This could be the answer. Oxfam gets dozens of stuffed bin bags every day. Ours probably won't be opened for a couple of weeks by which time nobody will know where it came from in the first place.

Tom Are you totally bonkers?! Sooner or later those poor old dears at Oxfam will open our bin bag expecting to find a moth-eaten cardigan and a pair of old shoes — not a chopped-up gall-bladder and a pair of smelly feet!

He pushes Harry out through the door

Harry exits

(*Yelling after him*) And you phone me the second you get that bin bag back! (*To Dick*) And *you*, give me that mobile!

As Dick hands Tom the mobile, from upstairs comes the sound of a trumpet playing — not wonderfully well — "Prepare Your Boat For Sailing"

(*Reacting*) What the bloody — ?!

Dick That's Granddad. He plays the trumpet.

Tom Oh, my God!

Dick His pretty granddaughter was telling me (*miming*) her granddad is the leading light in the local town band and in his younger days he was a "star" of "stage", "screen" and "radio".

Tom I don't care!

Dick I think that's what her mime meant. Either that or he was a train driver on the Kosovan underground railway.

Andreas appears, playing the trumpet with one hand and holding an open bottle of brandy in the other. Andreas finishes with a flourish

Andreas Geezooar! [Cheers!] GEZUAR! (*He swigs from the bottle and then sings an up-beat version of "I Want To Be Happy" — the only English word he knows is "happy". During the song, he dances to the sofa and collapses on to it. Singing*) "La-la-la-la happy. La-la-la-la-happy. La-la-la-la-Happy doo" (*During the following, he continues to play the odd note on the trumpet*)

Tom (*to Dick*) He's pissed!

Dick Yeah, I introduced the old boy to my fags and brandy.

Tom You tit!

Dick No, least I could do. (*Miming*) From what the "pretty granddaughter" says "Granddad" hasn't had a "drink" since 1997. (*He finishes "1997" with five fingers of one hand and two of the other*)

Tom I'll give you 1997. (*He finishes his mime with a two finger V sign*) Hold that.

Tom gives the piece of paper to Dick to hold so that Tom can dial. Dick immediately lowers the piece of paper to talk

Dick Oh, I forgot to tell you. (*Miming*) Pretty granddaughter explained. That telephone number belongs to her mummy in Shepherd's Bush. (*Pointing to Andreas*) Pretty granddaughter's mummy is his daughter.

Tom As long as they collect them right now I don't care who they are. (*To Andreas*) Shut up!

Katerina appears on the landing

Katerina Joohsh! Boll mee! Joosh! [Granddad! Stop that! Granddad!] GJYSH! BOLL ME! GJYSH! (*She rushes to him*) Joohsh! [Granddad!] GJYSH!

Tom (*snatching the piece of paper from Dick*) Give me that! (*He starts to dial*)

Dick (*to Katerina, miming*) We're ringing Mummy.

Katerina (*to Andreas, excitedly*) Aye po teleefoanon maameen! [He is telephoning Mummy!] AI PO TELEFONEN MAMIN!

Andreas (*to Dick*) Vizjaa eemah ae mreckoolooashmae! Tee nae teleefon. [My beautiful daughter! You telephone.] VAJZA IME E MREKUL-LUESHME! TI NE TELFON.

Dick Yes. Lovely, eh? (*To Andreas*) Soon you will be in *Shepherd's Bush*.

Andreas Eyo, eyo. Sheepherd's Bowsh. [No, no *Sheepherd's Bowsh*.] JO, JO SHEEPHERDS BOWSH.

Dick Please yourself, Sheepherd's Bowsh. With your daughter.

Andreas Eyo, eyo. *Dowter. Dowter. Sheepherd's Bowsh*.

Dick OK. Dowter, Sheepherd's Bowsh!

Tom Shut up (*On the mobile*) Hallo! Who am I speaking to please? ... No, you'll have to speak English. ... No, you'll have to — (*To Katerina*) I think *you* might speak their lingo. It's a lady.

Tom hands her the mobile

Dick Dowter, Sheepherd's Bowsh!
Andreas Dowter! (*He happily moves to Katerina*)
Katerina (*on the mobile, apprehensively*) Alloe [Hallo? ...] ALO (*Yelling happily*) Marmee! Marmee! Yetee Marmee! [Mama! Mama. It's you! Mama!!] MAMI! MAMI, JETI MIAMI! (*To Dick*) Marmee! [Mama!] MAMI! (*To Tom*) Marmee! [Mama!] MAMI! (*To Andreas*) Marmee! [Mama!] MAMI! Po, yarmee na Londer. [Yes, we're here in London.] PO, JEMI NE LONDER.

Katerina looks lovingly to Andreas. During the following, she starts to cry with emotion

(*On the mobile*) Po. Po. Jooshy ershter. [Yes, Yes. Granddad is here.] PO. PO. GJYSHI ESHTE. Oh, Marmee, Marmee! Ta dooah me kah maaree mallee! Nook mond ta besay ta do tay te show I dote eerie me to! [Oh, Mama, Mama! I love you! I've missed you! I can't believe I'm going to see you and be with you!] OH, MAMI, MAMI! TE DUAl! ME KA MARRE MALLI! NUK MUND TA BESOJ QE DO TE TE SHOH, E DO YE ERRI ME TY! Oo bay ko-ay ee jatay nook mendoya say doe tay seeyar perseriee, marmee mamie-ya eemay ee reckoolooloo-eshmay! [It's been so long! I thought I was never going to see you again. Mama, my beautiful Mama!] U BE KOHE E GJATE! NUK MENDOJA SE DO TE SHIHJA PERSERI, MAMI, MAMAJA IME E MREKULLUESHME!

She is now sobbing uncontrollably. She hands the phone to Andreas and sits beside him. During the following, Dick feels for a handkerchief, can't find one so looks to Tom who tersely produces a hanky which Dick passes to Andreas. Andreas blows his nose and hands the hanky back to Dick who passes it to Tom who snatches it back

Andreas (*starting to laugh and cry*) May dookayt ay pabaysooayshee tay takoyah pairsairee paas jeethee kaytiray vitayvee. Beeyah eemay ay mrekoollooayshmay. [I can't believe I will be seeing you after all these years. My beautiful girl.] ME DUKEY E PABESUESHME TE TAKOJA PERSERI PAS GJITHE KETYRE VITEVE. BIJA IME E MREKUL-LUESHME. (*Sobbing*) Ay mrekoollooayshmay eemay ... [My beautiful ...] E MREKULLUESHMJA IME ... (*On the mobile now weeping* *uncontrollably*) Nay Kaymee pritour kack hyatee per kaytee moment tay cmour. Kaj gyatee — kaj gyatee — [We have waited so long for this precious moment. So very — so very —] NE KEMI PRITUR KAQ GJATE PER KETE MOMENT TE CMUAR. KAQ GJATE — KAQ GJATE ——

Andres hands a blank-faced Dick the mobile. During the following, Katerina comforts Andreas

Dick (*on the mobile*) Hallo, Mama! ... I didn't quite get that but you're speaking to Dick. Our address is 25 Larkhall Lane, Kennington. So, if you don't know the short cut through Fulham and Battersea, come straight through Maida Vale to Hyde Park Corner and down the Mall to Buckingham Palace. You know Buckingham Palace where Queen Elizabeth lives. You know the Queen! (*In a high voice*) My husband and I ——
Tom Never mind the short cut!
Dick Any problems, you ring my mobile. Here come number. 07768 625 521 ... 521, you got it. Now if for any reason it's switched off ... You can leave a message or text me ——
Tom (*interrupting*) Give it here! (*He grabs the phone. On the mobile*) You come now! Collecto pronto! (*He switches the mobile off*)
Dick Should be here in twenty minutes from Sheepherd's Bowsh.

Tom thrusts the mobile at Dick

Katerina (*still overcome*) Oh, falimindairit! Falimindairit! [Oh, thank you! Thank you!] OH, FALEMINDERIT! FALEMINDERIT!

She kisses Tom passionately. Dick taps Katerina's shoulder

Dick (*to Katerina, miming as he speaks*) I was actually the one who drove the van, you know. (*He offers his face to be kissed*)
Katerina Fallimindairit! Falimindairit! [Thank you! Thank you!] FALEMINDERIT! FALEMINDERIT!

She kisses him passionately

Andreas Fallimindairit Falimindairit! [Thank you! Thank you!] FALEMINDERIT! FALEMINDERIT!

Andreas starts to kiss Tom

Tom Save that for your dowter in Sheepherd's Bowsh! (*To Andreas and Katerina*) Back upstairs the pair of you!

He turns Katerina but she grabs Dick's arm

Katerina (*to Dick*) Mo greeo ooriar! Tee the dohy zheehar port a gren! [I am starving! You said you were getting food!] ME GRIIU URIQ! TI THE DOTE GJEJE PER TE NGRENE!
Dick Oh, yeah, sorry! Phoning Mama put it right out of my head.
Tom Now what?!
Dick (*miming*) Well, the pretty granddaughter explained that she and granddad hadn't eaten for two days so I said you'd make 'em a sandwich.
Tom (*exasperated*) Look, I'm more worried about Mrs Potter and Harry's bin bag than their bloody sandwiches.
Dick (*to Katerina*) I think you'd better make your own sandwich. (*Pointing*) Kitchen through there.
Katerina Ah, Koozheener! Koozheener! [Kitchen! Kitchen!] KUZHINA! KUZHINA!

Katerina runs into the kitchen, shutting the door behind her

Tom (*starting to follow*) Never mind the kuzhina!
Andreas Koozheener! Koozheener! [Kitchen! Kitchen.] KUZHINA! KUZHINA. (*He leaps into a Cossack dancing routine*)
Tom Stop that! (*To Dick*) You! Lock Dizzy Gillespie upstairs. He's staying there until Mama arrives and takes him off to Shepherd's Bush.
Andreas (*correcting him*) No! Shepherd's Bowsh!

Andreas suddenly falls to one knee and does an impression of Al Jolson singing "California Here I Come" — but replacing the lyrics with "Sheepherd's Bowsh"

(*Singing*) Sheepherd's, Sheepherd's Sheepherd's Bowsh. Sheepherd's, Sheepherd's Sheepherd's Bowsh. My Dowter, my dowter, Shee-heeperd's Bowsh, My dowter —— !
Tom (*interrupting*) Shut your cake-hole! (*To Dick*) Get this nutcase upstairs.
Andreas Nowt-kays! More brandy!

Dick takes him upstairs

Dick Come on, Granddad.
Andreas Growndaid! Great Britain! (*To Dick*) Me love Tony Blairy!
Dick Yes, we all do!
Andreas You Tony Blairy?
Dick No, me Dicky Kerwood!
Andreas Me love Dicky.

Dick Yes, we all do.

Dick takes Andreas off upstairs

Tom hurries to the kitchen and opens the door

Tom (*calling*) Oy, they're Mrs Potter's sandwiches!

The cordless phone rings. Tom slams the kitchen door closed

(*To himself*) Please be Harry! (*He lifts the cordless phone. On the phone*) Hallo? ... Harry! Did you get to the Oxfam shop before Alfie? ... Thank God for that! ... What? ... What do you mean, "You discussed it with Alfie?!" ... (*Exploding*) You told him what was in the bin bags?! ... I don't care what contacts Alfie has, just get that bin bag to the dump in Clapham!

Behind him, Downs pokes his head round the partly-open door. During the following, Downs makes a vague attempt to attract Tom's attention whilst walking down to Tom's side

(*On the phone*) Listen you dumbbell! ... No, shut up! Just go to Clapham right this bloody minute. ... Don't you dare! I do not want it back in my house!

Downs gently taps Tom on the shoulder. Tom turns

(*Turning to Downs*) Piss off! (*He turns back, not realizing he's addressing Downs, and continues his tirade. On the phone*) So you just bloody do what I tell you! No messing! Right now! (*He suddenly realizes. He slowly turns, blankly to Downs. On the phone, pleasantly*) No messing! Right now take your smelly dog walkies to Clapham ... No, I have not been sniffing formaldehyde, bye bye. (*He replaces the phone. Cheerfully to Downs*) Family! What can I do for you, Constable?
Downs Sorry to disturb you, sir, but I forgot to ask you and your wife something.
Tom Well, you can ask me, the wife's not in.

Katerina walks through from the kitchen eating a thick sandwich. She stops on seeing Downs

Downs points to Katerina and indicates that she is in

(*Happily*) She is now! She wasn't a second ago. She was in there. (*He points to the kitchen*) Now she's in here. Yes. I've locked the — er — because she's finished her — er — so I've given her — er — yes.

Downs is looking confused

So you were saying you forgot to ask us something, Constable.
Downs Yes. Silly thing to forget really. Your name.
Tom You've forgotten your name.

Tom takes Downs away from Katerina and behind his back indicates for Katerina to go

Downs No. I forgot to ask you yours. For the incident report.
Tom It's Thomas Kerwood.

Katerina tiptoes towards the kitchen

Downs (*writing*) Middle name?
Tom George.
Downs (*writing*) I've already got the address, Mr Kerwood.

He turns to Katerina who he now sees in the kitchen doorway

(*Calling*) Madam!

She scuttles to beside them, closing the kitchen door behind her

What's your first name, Mrs Kerwood?

He prepares to write the name in his notebook. Katerina looks scared. Downs looks up at her

(*Louder*) Your first name, madam?

She looks more scared

(*Louder*) Your first ——— !
Tom (*interrupting, rightly*) My wife doesn't speak English.

Downs looks surprised

Her first name is — Adriatica.

Downs looks at Tom blankly for a moment

Downs (*writing*) Adriatica. (*He looks up*) Middle name?

Tom Armenia.

Downs gives Tom another blank look

Downs (*finally starting to write*) Adriatica Armenia Kerwood.
Tom Unusual, isn't it?

Downs looks up briefly

(*Babbling on*) I met her on holiday. She was a ski instructor in Gdansk. She refused to learn English! So I refused to learn to ski! (*He mimes skiing. Getting hysterical*) Apart from that we have a bloody good time. (*He mimes the pelvic thrust. To Downs*) They're dead sexy in Gdansk.

Katerina is now looking scared

(*To Katerina*) Don't look so worried, Adriatica.
Katerina (*frightened and not understanding*) Adriatica?
Tom Adriatica Armenia. Little wifey from Gdanski.

He chucks her under the chin. She backs away in fear

He's a nice policeman. Evening all! (*He mimes a bobby swinging a truncheon*) Not nasty ... (*Miming a police siren*) Wah, wah, wah, wah.

Katerina looks more scared

I think you should go now, Officer. Adriatica's a bit upset this morning. She's had some distressing news.

Tom turns Downs to go but Downs turns back

Downs What was that then?
Tom Eh? Oh, My — er ... mother-in-law died.

Tom moves Downs to go but Downs moves to Katerina.

Downs (*to Katerina*) Oh, I'm sorry to hear that, madam.
Tom (*quickly*) We all are. (*To Katerina*) The constable says — (*sadly*) sorryski Mumski dieski. (*He indicates for Downs to go*)
Downs Can't have been all that old.
Tom No, she wasn't. (*To Katerina. More sad*) Not oldski, Mumski, dieski.

Tom starts to cry and indicates for Katerina to join in. She is confused, but does a very quick wail. Tom indicates for Downs to go

Downs Was it sudden? You know, her mother ——
Tom This morning! (*To Katerina, even more sad*) Suddenski Mumski dieski.

Tom cries more and indicates for Katerina to join in. She does another brief loud wail. Tom then indicates for Downs to go

Downs Just er — just how did your mother-in-law die?
Tom (*weeping*) She was hit by a bus in Brixton!

Tom moves Downs to the front door

Downs Hit by a bus. Oh, that's terrible!
Tom (*wiping his eyes*) Yes. I think you should goski, nowski, pleaseski.
Downs Yes, I think maybe I will. And that rear door of your van is still open. There's a lot of young villains round here.
Tom Yes, you can't trust anybody these days.
Downs I'll — er — say good-morning then.
Tom (*sadly*) And you said it very niceski.

Without thinking, Tom puts the plate of sandwiches in Downs' hand

Downs rather awkwardly exits through the front door, with the plate of sandwiches

Tom closes the door and buries his head in his hands

Dick's head appears around the corner of the stairs

Dick Ohh, Dad would have been so proud of youski.

Tom lowers his hands and glares at Dick

(*To Katerina*) And you were brilliant, darling, with the old (*wailing suddenly*) Mumski dieski. (*To Tom*) And I meant to say. She told me her name is Katerina. Beautiful, isn't it? Katerina? Much better than Adriatica Armenia.
Tom *Go* and lock that van of mine before that copper starts snooping around amongst your bloody boxes.

Dick Good thinking.
Harry (*off*) Coming through!

Harry wheels the wheelbarrow in through the kitchen door

Tom is aghast as Harry tips the bin bag on to the floor

Tom What the bloody hell —— ?!
Harry I know what you said, Tom, but Alfie has come up with the greatest
scheme!
Tom It's going to the dump in Clapham!
Katerina Chfar eshtay kee-o? [What is that?] CFARE ESHTE KJO?
Tom Don't even ask!
Harry (*to Katerina*) Oo, you must be the pretty granddaughter.
Dick Katerina from Kosova.
Harry (*sexily*) Harry from Haringay.
Dick (*to Katerina*) Harry from Haringay not as nice as Dickie from
Docklands.
Tom Shut up! (*To Harry*) Get that to Clapham! (*To Dick*) You, lock the
bloody van.
Dick Let's hear Alfie's scheme. He's had some bloody good ones in his day.
Tom Alfie has just spent six months in the nick for fiddling his VAT.
Dick There's always a downside.
Tom Go and ——
Dick (*interrupting*) Lock the bloody van, right.

Dick exits through the front door

Tom (*to Harry*) And you get that back in the barrow!
Harry Just listen will you?
Tom I swear to God I'll kill you, Harry.
Harry Tom, if we dump it in Clapham we won't earn a penny.
Tom I don't want to earn a penny! Now lift!

They start to get hold of the bin bag

Harry Listen, will you. Alfie reckons there are lots of student doctors who
don't get enough body parts to practise on and the going rate is £45 a head.
Tom (*yelling*) Harry! In the barrow! One — two!

They are just about to lift the bin bag into the wheelbarrow

*Andreas appears on the landing. He is even more drunk. He carries a half-
empty bottle of brandy and is playing his trumpet to the tune of "California
Here I Come"*

Tom and Harry, startled, drop the bin bag and turn to look at Andreas

Katerina Joosh! [Granddad!] GJYSH! (*She rushes to Andreas*)
Tom (*determined*) OK! One, two, three.

On three, Dick enters from the front door

Dick Tom — !
Tom
Harry } (*together, startled*) Ahh!

They turn, miss the wheelbarrow and drop the bin bag on to the floor

Tom What?!
Dick Getting out of a car … !
Tom What? Who?
Dick Looks like your Mrs Potter.
Tom Bloody hell! Stall her for a couple of minutes.
Dick How?!
Tom Tell her a funny story.
Dick Right. I'll tell her the one about the two nuns and the donkey.

Dick exits through the front door

Tom (*to Katerina, miming*) You and Granddad upstairs till Mama come from Sheepherd's Bowsh.
Andreas (*immediately singing*) Sheepherd's, Sheepherd's, Sheepherd's Bowsh —— (*As he sings he dances above the sofa-bed as though making a stage exit*)
Tom Bloody hell! (*To Katerina*) Grab him!
Katerina Joosh! [Granddad!] GJYSH!

She chases him but, en route, he picks up the handles of the empty wheelbarrow just as Tom and Harry and are preparing to lift the bin bag into it

Tom Right. One, two ——

Andreas, pushes the wheelbarrow past them, singing. They are left holding the bin bag

The singing Andreas pushes the wheelbarrow out through the open kitchen door

Tom } (*yelling together*) { Oy!
Harry   { Come back!
Katerina Joosh! Poosha! [Granddad! Stop!] GJYSH! PUSHO!

As Katerina exits after Andreas, Dick hurries in through the front door

Dick She's coming and she doesn't have a sense of humour!
Tom The kitchen!
Harry The window!

Tom moves above the chair towards the kitchen and Harry moves below the chair towards the window. As they are both holding the bin bag the bag splits down the middle and the contents spill on to the floor. In addition to the four Sainsbury's bags are several packages wrapped in hospital gauze. Some items are clearly recognizable as arms and legs — others are floppy parcels of various sizes. (NB. As yet we don't see the wrapped head!) The three of them react to the smell

Dick }   (Bloody hell!
Tom } (*together*) { Quick!!
Harry }   (Oh my God!

They each drop to their knees and start desperately trying to shove everything back into the split bin bag

Mrs Potter, clutching a briefcase, enters through the open front door. She is a formidable lady in her early fifties. She sees the three of them on the floor

Mrs Potter (*happily, positive*) Mrs Potter!

They turn to her horrified. Each is holding a body part

Music. Black-out

CURTAIN

ACT II

The same. Immediately following

The action is continuous so Stage Management must stop the clock during the interval

Mrs Potter Morning! Mrs Potter from the Agency. (*She moves down and holds out her hand. The smell suddenly hits*) Oh, that smell!
Tom (*sniffing*) Yes, quite nice, isn't it?

Tom frantically indicates for Dick and Harry to get rid of the body parts as he walks up to Mrs Potter attempting to convey that all is perfectly normal. During the following, he takes her coat off and hangs it up

(*Proffering his hand*) Thomas Kerwood Esquire. And I can't tell you how absolutely thrilled my wife and I are about today. It is such a joyous moment in our lives. If you'll just wait in the dining-room.

Tom gently starts to push Mrs Potter nearer the dining-room door

Harry We need a new bin bag!

Harry rushes into the kitchen

Tom (*gaily, to Mrs Potter*) Need a new bin bag. (*Importantly*) "Bin bags should be kept out of reach of babies and small infants for fear of suffocation."

Harry dashes back in from the kitchen with a large bin liner and 2 aerosol air fresheners

Harry One bin bag!

During the following, he and Dick shove the bits and pieces and the four Sainsbury bags into the bin-liner, tie the top and give a quick squirt with the air fresheners

Mrs Potter (*aghast*) They look like parts of a human body!
Tom (*to Mrs Potter*) It's all in hand. I'll show you into the dining-room.

The wrapped head of the body is dropped by the panicking Harry with a thump and gently rolls towards Tom. It stops at his feet. He smiles at Mrs Potter then picks it up and neatly throws it into the bin liner which is being held open by Dick

Tom Heads! (*Politely, to Mrs Potter*) If you'll just wait in the ——
Mrs Potter (*firmly*) Mr Kerwood —— !
Tom (*politely*) Mrs Potter?
Mrs Potter Are they or are they not parts of ... ?

She stops having seen something on the floor. She bends down and picks the something up. She stands and shows Tom: two small lemons. Tom nods, takes them and throws them at Harry who heads them neatly into the bin liner

Tom (*to Mrs Potter*) The dining-room ...

He goes to move her but she has now seen Harry, with difficulty, shoving what is clearly a wrapped foot into the bin liner

Mrs Potter (*pointing in horror*) That is definitely a foot!
Tom Well, give or take a couple of inches.

During the following, Tom gently eases her towards the dining-room

(*Wildly*) Now, if you'll just wait in there and think about all those questions you want to ask me. (*Desperate*) Oh, we'll make wonderful parents. I'll be a fantastic father!

She stops

Mrs Potter (*firmly*) Mr Kerwood!
Tom Mrs Potter!

By now Dick and Harry are tying the top of the bin bag

Mrs Potter What are human remains doing in your living-room?

Tom adopts an overly light-hearted manner

Tom Oh! Is that what's worrying you? Ah, no! They're imitation.
Mrs Potter Imitation?
Tom They are very well designed *replicas* — for the rehearsal.
Mrs Potter (*surprised*) Rehearsal?
Tom (*to Dick and Harry*) Take five, boys.

Dick and Harry rush towards the kitchen with the bin liner

*The kitchen door opens and Katerina pushes the wheelbarrow in. Andreas
is sitting in it playing "I Feel Pretty" on his trumpet*

*Dick grabs Andreas and yanks him out of the wheelbarrow. For Mrs Potter's
benefit Dick joyfully sings "I Feel Pretty' (as though part of the rehearsal)
and dances Andreas to the stairs. At the same time Harry joins in the singing,
grabs Katerina and dances her to the stairs*

Katerina and Andreas scuttle off upstairs

*Dick and Harry, still singing and dancing, put the bin bag into the wheel-
barrow. Dick opens the kitchen door*

*Harry pushes the wheelbarrow off. Harry returns. He and Dick bow as
their performance ends and they exit into the kitchen, closing the door*

*Mrs Potter has watched all this with wide-eyed bewilderment. She turns
enquiringly to Tom*

Not bad for a rehearsal. Old boy in the wheelbarrow a little bit over the top,
maybe.

Mrs Potter What on earth are they rehearsing?

Tom (*madly thinking*) They — are — rehearsing — (*brightly*) a reality TV
programme.

Mrs Potter Reality television programme?

Tom (*enthusiastically*) Yep. Great new idea.

Mrs Potter But how can imitation body parts and that unpleasant
smell ——?

Tom (*interrupting*) Ah, the smell! Isn't that clever? A mixture of formaldehyde, pesticide and fratricide.

Mrs Potter Formaldehyde, pesticide and —— ?

Tom (*interrupting*) Makes it really authentic, don't you think?

Mrs Potter But what kind of reality TV programme —— ?

Tom (*interrupting, wagging a knowing finger at her*) Ah! The idea of this
particular reality TV programme is — Shakespeare.

Mrs Potter Shakespeare?

Tom Yes. The Bard of — er — Shakespeare. Channel 4 — who are making
the reality TV programme — thought it was about time this reality rubbish
had a touch of culture. So, the idea is — to get ordinary families to perform
a Shakespeare play! No professionals involved. Direct it yourselves.
Choose your own play. I think it could be a winner.

He moves her towards the dining-room but she marches back

Mrs Potter So they were all part of your family. (*She waves in general directions*)

Tom My very extended family, yes!

Mrs Potter And which Shakespeare have you chosen?

Tom William, he's the best. (*Realizing*) Oh, which *play* of — er — ! *Titus* — er ——

Mrs Potter (*impressed*) *Titus Andronicus*.

Tom That's the one.

Mrs Potter An interesting choice.

Tom We thought so.

Mrs Potter Very good. Lots of blood.

Tom Yes.

Mrs Potter Hence the ... ?

Tom Hence the body parts — yes.

Mrs Potter But the old gentleman in the wheelbarrow.

Tom Uncle Bert, yes. He's a bit hammy, isn't he, with the ... (*he mimes a doddery old boy drinking*)

Mrs Potter Where exactly does that character fit into *Titus Andronicus*?

Tom He's playing the brother, Titus Anute. (*He laughs*) Uncle Bert thought he'd jolly the play up a bit. Bit of music and dancing.

Mrs Potter Well, if you're preparing your television programme, we should reschedule our meeting for a later date.

Tom No! Channel 4 want everything to be as normal as possible. Life goes on, all that stuff. You wait in the dining-room. I'll bring the coffee.

As he moves her towards the dining-room the telephone rings

Excuse me. (*He picks up the receiver. On the phone, happily*) Hallo? ... (*Even happier*) Hallo, darling! (*To Mrs Potter. Cheerfully*) It's my wife.

Mrs Potter (*surprised*) Your wife?

Tom (*on the phone*) You're at Mrs Potter's office. (*To Mrs Potter, laughing*) She's at your office.

Mrs Potter My office?

Tom (*on the phone*) No, the meeting's here, sweetheart. ... No the secretary is absolutely right. The meeting's *here*. ... Yes, I *know* that but Mrs Potter's turned up *here*! ... (*Very cheerful*) Now that's not a very nice thing to call Mrs ... (*He looks at Mrs Potter and laughs. Still cheerful*) Yes, we'll look forward to seeing you. No problems here. Bye, darling. (*He happily replaces the receiver*) We'll have a nice cup of coffee and start, shall we?

Mrs Potter (*surprised, indignantly*) I can't possibly begin the interview without Mrs Kerwood being present.

Tom She'll only be ten minutes. (*Indicating the dining-room*) I'll bring the coffee. We've got sandwiches. Cake. Bickies!

Mrs Potter I have other prospective parents to see today, you know. This is most inconvenient.

Tom I'm really very sorry. Total misunderstanding. (*He opens the dining-room door*) If you'll wait in the dining-room. Quieter in there. Away from the rehearsals. (*Projecting*) *Oh for a muse of fire, that is the question, Brutus! Perchance to dream and sleep no more, Ophelia!*

Mrs Potter is slightly taken aback by Tom's performance

I think it's very important for toddlers to grow up with an appreciation of drama, don't you?

Mrs Potter Well, yes, I do.

Tom All this eeney meeney miny mo' stuff. What kids want is — (*He does hunchback acting*) "Now is the winter of our discontent made glorious summer ..." (*Quickly*) I'll get the coffee.

Tom turns Mrs Potter to push her into the dining-room

A frantic Harry appears at the window

Harry The shit has hit the fan!

A surprised Mrs Potter looks to Tom

Tom We're doing the modern version. (*To Harry*) Try the entrance again, Titus, more gusto! (*To Mrs Potter*) Won't keep you a moment.

A bemused Mrs Potter goes into the dining-room

Tom slams the door and leans against it, drained as Harry clambers in and dashes towards the kitchen

(*Hoarsely*) What the hell's happened now?

Harry opens the kitchen door

An out-of-breath Dick rushes in pushing the wheelbarrow still containing the bin liner

Harry slams the door shut and Dick sits in the armchair DL *trying to catch his breath. Tom crosses to them*

(*Aghast. To Dick*) That's supposed to be in Harry's car on its way to Clapham!

Dick, breathless, waves his hand unable to speak

(*To Dick*) Why isn't it in that dump in Clapham?!

Dick, breathless, waves his hand unable to speak

(*To Dick*) What the bloody hell's happened?
Harry Why don't you ask me?

Tom glares at Harry

Tom (*icily to Harry*) Why isn't it in that dump in Clapham?

Dick has got his breath back before Harry can answer

Dick Policeman.
Tom (*suddenly scared*) Policeman?
Harry Same one.
Tom Same policeman?! You mean the one ... (*He points to the front door*)
Dick The one you were so clever with, yeah. He was in the back street checking out Harry's car. (*He points out of the window*)
Tom God!
Dick Well, we come tearing out the garden gate with the wheelbarrow, didn't we? And he's looking on the windscreen for Harry's tax disc ——
Harry (*interrupting*) I was definitely going to get it taxed and insured tomorrow.
Tom You —— !
Harry And I'm booked in for a driving test next month, honest.

Tom throws his hands in the air

Dick Well, we're stuck on the pavement with the wheelbarrow.
Harry So — rather cleverly — I said we were your gardeners.
Tom Gardeners?!
Harry (*pointing to the bin bag*) And this was garden stuff.
Tom What about the car?
Dick That's OK, we said it was yours.

Tom tries to control himself

Harry (*to Tom*) Give us a quick up-date on what's happened since that Potter woman arrived.
Dick Yeah.

Tom (*tersely*) You want a quick up-date?! (*Angrily and in one breath*) The Kerwood family is rehearsing a reality TV programme for Channel 4 which is a modern version of *Titus Andronicus* hence the body parts which are of course well designed replicas as is the appalling smell which comprises formaldehyde, pesticide and fratricide, all of which will be shown on Channel 4 on a date to be decided with God knows who as Titus Andronicus and Uncle Bert as Titus Anute.

There is a slight beat

Dick ⎫
Harry ⎭ (*together*) Very good!

They shake the furious Tom's hand and pat him on the back. The doorbell goes. They react

Harry It's that copper!
Tom Might not be!
Dick Yes, he said he wanted another word with you.

Katerina rushes in from upstairs

Katerina You luten ma indamoany! [Please help!] JU LUTEM ME NDIHMONI (*Pointing upstairs*) Jooshy eem! [My grandfather!] GJYSHI IM!
Tom (*to Katerina*) Ssh! (*Pointing*) Go back upstairs!
Katerina Eyo. Jooshy eem ushtar shoom ee simore! [No. My grandfather is being very sick!] JO. GJYSHI IM ESHTE SHUME I SEMURE!
Tom (*not understanding*) What the bloody hell's she saying?
Dick God knows!
Katerina Jooshy eem! [My grandfather!] GJYSHI IM! (*She points upstairs then does a quick doddery old boy mime*) Po vee-ell. [Is being sick.] PO VJELL. (*She does a graphic mime of Granddad vomiting*)
Dick (*to Tom*) That means her granddad's being sick.
Tom Thank you! (*To Katerina. Yelling*) He's drunk a bottle of brandy! I'm not surprised he's ... (*He mimes vomiting*)

The doorbell goes again, more urgently

(*To Harry*) Look if that copper's at the front, get that (*pointing to the wheelbarrow*) through the back quick.
Harry It's still a bit chancy, isn't it?
Tom Clear off!

A wan Andreas enters from upstairs. He carries a bottle of brandy which is a quarter full

Andreas Yam ketch! [I feel sick!] JAM KEQ!
Katerina Jooshy. [Grandfather.] GJYSHI.

Katerina hurries to him

Andreas Yam ketch! [I feel sick!] JAM KEQ!
Tom (*to Dick*) Just get him upstairs! (*To Harry*) And I don't want to see you again till you get back from Clapham!
Harry (*pointing to the bin liner*) If we'd buried him with the lemons he'd have disintegrated by now.
Tom Bugger off!

Harry exits into the kitchen with the wheelbarrow

Andreas Yam ketch! [I feel sick!] JAM KEQ!

During the following, he staggers to the back of the sofa-bed and collapses over it

Katerina Aye doata vee-ell persen. [He wants to be sick again.] AI DO TE VJELLE PERSEN. (*She graphically mimes vomiting again*)
Dick (*to Tom, miming*) Yam ketch means he wants to be sick again.
Tom I can tell that! (*To Dick*) Up to your flat. Call down from the window. See if you can get rid of that copper.
Dick How, for God's sake?
Tom Tell him a funny story.
Dick Right. How about: Why did the Mexican throw his wife off a cliff? Tequila!

Dick hesitates then quickly exits upstairs

Andreas Yam ketch! [I feel sick!] JAM KEQ!
Tom (*to Katerina*) Quick! (*Miming doddery old boy*) Get Granddad into that bedroom (*he points*) — be sick in loo.

Tom and Katerina lift the moaning Andreas

Mrs Potter appears in the dining-room doorway

Mrs Potter Mr Kerwood ——

Tom   ⎫ (*together*) Ahhh!
Katerina ⎭

Tom and Katerina drop the moaning Andreas and he flops back over the sofa-bed

Tom We've just got to Uncle Bert's murder scene.
Mrs Potter I'm thinking we should forget about the coffee.
Tom No, it's on the way.
Mrs Potter Time's getting on, Mr Kerwood.

A frantic Harry enters from the kitchen pushing the wheelbarrow containing the bin liner

Harry That copper's coming through the back gate! (*He dumps the bin bag on the floor by the sofa-bed, then freezes as he sees Mrs Potter*)
Tom (*to Mrs Potter*) This is the exciting bit!

Tom closes the dining-room door on her

Mrs Potter exits

Tom rushes to open the bedroom door

Harry I reckon he must have got fed up ringing the front door bell and has gone round the back.
Tom Well worked out, Harry.

Andreas is still flopped over the back of the sofa-bed

(*To Andreas*) Come on, you! (*To Katerina*) Give us a hand.

They lift up Andreas as Harry opens the sofa-bed and puts the bin bag into it

Katerina Jooshey! Jooshey!
Tom I'll give him Jooshey! Jooshey!
Andreas Yam ketch! [I feel sick!] JAM KEQ!
Tom Not half as ketch as I feel. (*To Harry*) Go stop that copper from …

Harry is heaving the bin bag into the open sofa-bed

What the hell are you doing?
Harry I'm hiding the evidence!

Harry slams the sofa-bed seat down but it catches the protruding top of the bin bag and springs open again. Harry bangs it down — it springs open again

Tom Bloody hell!

Tom and Harry together quickly shove the seat down. They hesitate — it stays

Right! (*Pointing to the kitchen*) Go and stop that copper! And I don't care how!

Harry I'll tell him one of Dick's funny stories! The one about the Irishman who fired an arrow into the air.

Harry exits into the kitchen, closing the door, and then immediately returns

And missed.

Harry rushes into the kitchen

Tom turns to Andreas who is being supported by Katerina

Tom (*to Andreas*) You — bedroom!

He about turns Andreas and throws him into the bedroom by the seat of his pants

Katerina Nook doohert ta ma trytony kooshtoo jooshy. (*She mimes a violent throw*) [That's no way to treat my grandfather.] NUK DUHET TE MA TRAJTONI KESHTU GIYSHIN.

Tom Shut your cake-hole!

He turns her but she turns back

Katerina Moss, ma berteet moo-ah, ashtoo! [Don't you shout at me like that!] MOS ME BERTIT MUA, ASHTU!

Tom Bless you!

He turns her and heaves her off

Katerina exits

Tom hurries away

Katerina immediately returns as a purposeful Downs backs Harry in from the kitchen

Tom and Katerina don't see Downs and Harry, who is smiling politely at Downs

Katerina Tsee goodsun termer traytosh kushtoo! [How dare you treat me like that!] SI GUXON TE ME TRAJTOSH KESHTU!

She mimes a violent throw as Tom hurries to her

Tom (*to Katerina*) Get back in there!

He turns her but she turns back

Katerina Traygoamar shooma respect per moo-ah geethastoo! [And show me some respect as well!] TREGOME SHUME RESPEKT PER MUE GJITHASHTU!

Harry, on seeing Downs, smiles politely at him and sits on the sofa-bed

Harry (*calling to Tom, politely*) Excuse me! Visitor!
Tom (*turning to Harry*) Shut up! (*To Katerina*) You just get back into that bedroom — ! (*He suddenly realizes that when he turned he saw Downs; to Katerina, his voice getting sweeter and more foolish*) You — get back — into that bedroom — Adriatica — wifey. (*He accompanies the rest of the speech with a convoluted sign language*) And you have nice *rest* — you need to *relax* before we buryski poorski Mumski. Let me deal with ... (*He indicates Downs*) Who is a nice — "Evening all". (*He mimes a happy bobby swinging a truncheon*) But I'm sure he can turn into (*miming a police siren*) wah wah wah wah.
Katerina OK!

Katerina scoots into the bedroom

Tom Sorry, Constable. It's been a difficult morning.
Downs I was waiting at that front door for ages.
Tom (*pleasantly*) Well, luckily you found the back way in.
Downs (*firmly*) According to your two gardeners ——
Tom Bradford and Bingley, yes. (*NB. Bradford & Bingley are a famous British mortgage lending company! For any production outside the UK please feel free to change to any business double act suitable to your territory*)

Downs hesitates but decides to ignore this

Downs — in addition to owning a white van you also ——

Dick rushes on to the landing from upstairs

Dick (*as he enters*) It's OK! There's no sign of that —— (*he stops on seeing Downs*) — there's no sign of that mildew or leaf-drop on the potted azalea. (*A beat*) I'll just go and check the winter pansies.

Dick rushes back upstairs

Tom (*after a brief pause, calling out*) Thank you, Bingley. You were saying, Constable?
Down (*getting terse*) Your two gardeners ——
Tom Bradford and Bingley, yes.
Downs (*pressing on*) — said that Ford fiesta parked out the back ——

The dining-room door opens and Mrs Potter enters carrying an office file

Mrs Potter (*entering, calling*) And no sugar for me!
Tom (*hurrying to Mrs Potter*) Right! Bit busy in here!
Mrs Potter (*moving to Downs*) Oh. Sorry to interrupt the rehearsal. Carry on, Constable. Or should I call you Titus. (*pronounced "Tight arse"*)

Tom nearly dies. Downs considers this for some time!

Downs (*finally*) I beg your pardon?
Tom No, he's not part of the — er … He's real — er … (*To Harry*) He's a real one, isn't he?
Harry (*rising*) Yeah, he's a real one. (*He sits*)
Downs (*to Mrs Potter*) Constable Downs.
Mrs Potter Oh, pardon me. A genuine member of the force. (*To Tom*) No problem in the Kerwood family, I trust.
Tom No, no, no, no, no.

He turns her but she turns back

Mrs Potter And is there any sign of Mrs Kerwood yet?
Tom No, no, no, no, no.

He turns her

Downs Just went into the bedroom, didn't she?

They turn to look at him

(*To Tom*) Didn't you just tell her to have a little rest in bed?

Mrs Potter (*surprised*) A little rest in —— ?!
Tom (*to Mrs Potter*) Oh, *that* Mrs Kerwood. My wife, Mrs Kerwood. I
thought you meant my *brother's* (*pointing to Harry*) wife, Mrs Kerwood.
Downs Your brother? I thought he was Bradford, the gardener.
Tom Correct. He's my gardener — and my brother. Bradford Kerwood. I
like to keep the odd jobs in the family, don't I, Bradford?

*Harry rises and decides to adopt a broad West Country accent which he feels
is more suitable for a gardener*

Harry Yeah, he's very good to me and Bingley.

Tom closes his eyes in anguish as Harry sits

Tom Bingley's my other brother — and my other gardener. So! I didn't
realize Mrs Potter meant any sign of *my* wife *Linda* — whose nickname is
Adriatica. I thought she meant any sign of Nellie — who's married to
Bradford. (*He points to Harry*)

Harry rises. Throughout the following he retains the West Country accent

Harry Yeah. My wife, Nellie. Who doesn't have a nickname. Bingley's not
married.

*Harry sits. Mrs Potter and Downs look confused. Tom is bemused by the
accent*

Tom Yes, I was just about to tell you that my wife has, in fact returned and
is resting in bed.
Mrs Potter (*annoyed*) But I need to meet the lady. She's already late for our
appointment.
Tom You wait in the dining-room. I'll wake her up right away.
Mrs Potter Wake her … ?! There's a lot of paperwork to complete, you
know. (*Hitting the file*) Numerous official forms. It's deadly serious what's
happening, Mr Kerwood!
Downs Are you from the undertakers, madam?

Tom nearly dies

Mrs Potter The undertakers?
Downs Only if you are I hope you'll show Mrs Kerwood a little more
consideration than what you're showing now.
Tom She's not from the undertakers! (*To Harry*) She's not from the
undertakers is she, Barnsley? (*Then quickly*) Bradford!
Harry No, not from the undertakers, sir — brother, sir.

Harry salutes and sits. Tom glares at him

Mrs Potter Why would an undertaker be required here?
Downs Mr Kerwood's mother-in-law was run over by a bus in Brixton this morning.

Tom sits beside Harry and holds his head in his hands

Sadly she's dead.
Mrs Potter (*to Tom*) Your mother-in-law … ?
Tom (*looking up*) Hit by a bus. Number 34. To Victoria. Right, Bradford?
Harry (*rising*) If you say so, sir!

Harry salutes and sits. Tom's glare is fiercer

Mrs Potter (*to Tom*) Why on earth didn't you tell me sooner?
Tom I didn't want you to think I was playing for sympathy.
Mrs Potter We should reschedule the meeting for a later date.
Tom (*quickly rising*) No!
Mrs Potter I'm worried about the time as it is!
Tom I'll get my wife out of bed and we'll be in right away.

He takes her to the dining-room door

Mrs Potter Please be quick.

He indicates for her to go into the dining-room. She stops

When's your mother-in-law's funeral?
Tom (*starting to weep*) Saturday. St Mary's. Four o'clock. No flowers. Just a contribution.

He sobs as he slams the dining-room door on her

Mrs Potter exits

He turns back, still sobbing, and wiping his eyes. Harry is looking at him blankly. Tom surreptitiously slaps the back of Harry's head to get him to join in. Harry goes into an immediate wail. Downs watches, deadpan. Harry emits a louder wail — then an even louder wail. Tom slaps Harry's head again. Harry immediately stops. Tom, wiping his eyes, moves to Downs

Sorry about that little show of emotion. Thanks for calling, Officer. You've been really helpful. Hasn't he been helpful, — er ——
Harry Bradford.

Tom Bradford.

Harry (*rising*) Very helpful, sir brother. (*He sits*)

Downs (*to Tom*) Hold it! I want to ask you a thing or two.

Tom Couldn't you come back tomorrow?

Downs No, I could not! I've been messed about here quite enough. Now! According to your two gardeners — (*quickly*) Bradford and Bingley — your two brothers — you own that Ford Fiesta out the back!

Tom Well, if that's what (*indicating Harry*) Bradford and Bingley said ——

Downs Well, do you?

Tom (*quickly*) Yes.

Downs (*flatly*) It doesn't have a tax disc.

Tom (*amazed*) My Ford Fiesta doesn't have a —— ?

Downs (*interrupting, angrily*) Look, normally I wouldn't give a monkey's about a tax disc but I'm beginning to think there's more to you than meets the eye, Mr Kerwood. You've already given me some cock and bull story about the white van out there and your wife's missing pussy!

Tom (*after a brief pause, amazed*) My Ford Fiesta doesn't have a tax disc?! Well, I just don't understand! I stuck it on myself. I don't mean I stuck it on myself. I mean I myself stuck it on the windscreen. (*Suddenly*) Of course! Must have come unstuck. (*To Harry*) Happened before, hasn't it — er ——

Downs (*flatly*) Bradford.

Tom Thank you. (*To Harry*) Bradford.

Harry rises

Harry (*still West Country*) Yes. Happened before, sir brother. The constable should have looked through the car window to see if the disc was on the floor. (*He sits*)

Downs I did, it isn't.

Tom Ah, under the seat. (*To Harry*) Bradford!

Harry (*standing up*) Yes, Mr brother Kerwood, sir?

Tom Escort the constable back to the car, will you? You've — er — already got the keys, haven't you?

Harry Yes, Mr Kerwood, sir brother, sir. Sir Kerwood, sir.

Downs I don't need to take a second —— !

Tom (*interrupting*) Yes, it's definitely there! (*To Harry, authoritatively*) You search that car thoroughly for that tax disc! It must be found. I don't care if it takes fifteen minutes. (*Pointedly*) Or even longer.

Downs I don't have all day, sir.

During the following, the seat of the sofa-bed springs up behind Tom and Downs. Harry sees it and tiptoes back to the sofa-bed, pushes the seat down, it springs up again. Harry quickly pushes it down and sits on the sofa-bed

Tom (*dramatically*) You have made a very serious charge, Constable, and, in this country, a man is still innocent until proven guilty. I have no criminal record whatsoever and I will not accept this slur on my good character. (*He turns to where Harry had been standing*) Bradford!

Tom is surprised that Harry is not where he was. He is even more surprised to see Harry sitting there on the sofa-bed

Bradford! Don't just sit there. Take the constable back to the car and search high and low for that tax disc!

There is a pause as Harry thinks what to do

Harry (*finally, belligerently*) I won't!

Tom is totally taken aback and moves a pace towards Harry

Tom (*floundering*) Go with the constable, Bradford!
Harry Won't.

Tom moves to Harry

Tom (*getting wilder*) Do as you're told, Bradford!

Tom lifts Harry up

Harry (*quickly sitting*) I won't!

Tom is totally confused

Tom (*at a loss*) For God's sake, Bradford!

He lifts him

Harry (*sitting*) No!
Tom (*pleading*) Bradford!!!
Harry Well, I will if you come and sit beside me first. (*He slides up the sofa-bed*)
Tom (*totally bemused*) What?
Harry I want you to sit beside me. Please! Like you used to when you, me and Bingley were kids. You used to cuddle up to your little brother — before I became your gardener. Please. (*He pats the seat*) Then Bradford will get up.

Tom looks awkwardly from Harry to the deadpan Downs, smiles and looks back to Harry

Tom Well, all right. If that's what you want, Bradford. (*He sits beside Harry*)
Harry Lovely. That's all I needed. A little bit of—intimacy—before I leave you. I'll go now.

Harry stands up and moves UR *behind the sofa-bed, never taking his eyes off Tom*

Harry (*to Tom, quickly*) Don't you move! Until we've gone. You stay there. (*He starts to edge towards Downs. To Tom*) Stay! I want to remember you just as you are. Sitting there.

He gently turns the expressionless Downs towards the kitchen door and, during the following, Harry slowly marches Downs through the kitchen door

(*Without taking his eyes off Tom*) With that special look on your face. Still. Like the morning breeze. Motionless, placid, tranquil. Ever peaceful.

Harry and Downs exit, closing the kitchen door

For a moment Tom is mesmerized. He then remembers Mrs Potter is waiting in the dining-room

Tom (*suddenly*) Coffee! (*He rushes towards the dining-room door and opens it. Calling in*) Did you say sugar or no sugar?!
Mrs Potter (*off, coldly*) No sugar, thank you!
Tom (*calling*) Sweet enough, eh? (*Not getting a reply he closes the door*)

As he rushes towards the kitchen the seat of the sofa-bed springs open

Oh, my God! (*He quickly slams it shut and starts to run to the kitchen as the seat springs open again*) God! (*He starts to hurry back towards the sofa-bed*)

Linda backs in through the front door, removing the front-door key

Linda (*entering*) Tom!

Tom dives headfirst over the sofa-bed and lounges in it in a state of relaxation. By this time, Linda has removed the front-door key, closed the door and turned

(*Breathing heavily*) Whew! Couldn't get — couldn't get a damn taxi.

Dick hurries on to the landing

Dick I just saw Linda get out of … ! (*He sees Linda. Pleasantly*) Hi, Linda!
(*He smiles*) Bye, Linda.

Dick rushes off again

*Linda gives a dismissive wave to the departed Dick. Hanging up her coat on
the hook* U *she turns to Tom who is sitting there, madly thinking, but looking
at her blankly*

Linda Where's — where's this wretched Mrs Potter then?

Tom hesitates

Stupid woman getting me all the way to her place then … (*She takes a deep
breath*) Ohh! So what's she like?

Tom hesitates

Has she asked you any questions yet?

Tom hesitates and then shakes his head

She's in the dining-room, is she?

Tom hesitates and then nods

Have you given her coffee and sandwiches?

Tom hesitates and then shakes his head

(*Getting terse*) Are you all right?

Tom hesitates and then gives a gesture of so-so with his hand

Well, go and sort out the coffee while I make myself presentable. I feel sick!
(*She moves towards the bedroom*)
Tom (*after a fractional pause*) No!!

*He leaps up and gets to the bedroom. During the following, he leans over the
back of the sofa-bed to make sure it doesn't spring open — whilst at the same
time preventing Linda from going towards the bedroom by holding his leg up
against the bedroom door*

Linda (*jumping*) God! What is it?
Tom You can't go in there!
Linda Why on earth not?

Tom It's occupied.
Linda What do you mean occupied?
Tom Occupied — occupied — occupied. By people.
Linda Who for God's sake?
Tom The plumber and his mate.
Linda (*astonished*) We've got the plumber in there?
Tom Water *everywhere*. Bathroom. Bedroom. I turned the bathroom tap on and it came off in my hand.
Linda What!?
Tom Yeah! Couldn't stop the flow. Woosh!

Tom takes his hands off the sofa-bed to mime a little woosh. Unseen by Linda, the seat of the sofa-bed pops up

(*Yelling*) Woosh!! (*He quickly shuts the seat*) And they don't want you in there while they're fixing it. You tidy yourself up in the kitchen.

As Linda heads for the kitchen Tom clambers over the sofa-bed and sits on it

Linda God, what a morning! Let's be quick then. I'll make myself presentable. You come and do the coffee. (*She holds out her hand for him to join her*)
Tom No, I'm staying here.
Linda You're what!?
Tom I've got to help the plumber in the bedroom.
Linda (*astonished*) Help the plumber?
Tom He can't find the stop-cock.
Linda Well go and show him!
Tom Yeah. (*He doesn't move*)
Linda Well, go on then.
Tom I'm just trying to remember where the stop-cock is.
Linda God! (*She turns to go into the kitchen but sees the wheelbarrow. Astonished*) What's this wheelbarrow doing in the living-room?
Tom I've been trying to work that one out, too.

Linda exits in despair into the kitchen

Tom rushes to the kitchen and goes to lock the door — no key. He frantically feels in his pockets

(*To himself*) Lock door with key. Where's the bloody key?! Linda's got it. (*He sees the wheelbarrow and quickly pushes it in front of the kitchen door, blocking it. He then rushes to the stairs. Calling*) Dick! Get down here! (*He then rushes to the bedroom door and opens it*) Oy! You two!

He runs into the bedroom closing the door as Dick's head appears around the top of the stairs and he looks around

Dick (*apprehensively*) Tom? (*He tiptoes downstairs*) Tom?

Mrs Potter enters from the dining-room

Mrs Potter Mr Kerwood, I've been waiting … ! (*She stops on seeing Dick*) Oh!
Dick (*at a loss*) Ah. Nice to see you again, Mrs Potty.
Mrs Potter Potter.
Dick Potter. I'm Mr Kerwood, by the way.
Mrs Potter Oh. You must be Bingley.

Dick looks blank

Dick Must I?
Mrs Potter Bradford's brother.
Dick (*blankly*) Bradford's brother. Oh, yeah! *That* Bingley.
Mrs Potter So you're a gardener as well.
Dick As well as what?
Mrs Potter As well as your brother.
Dick Brother Bradford, yeah?
Mrs Potter Well, your other brother employs you, doesn't he?
Dick Does he?
Mrs Potter As a gardener.
Dick I thought that was Bingley.
Mrs Potter (*angrily*) Mr Kerwood!
Dick Mrs Potty!
Mrs Potter Potter!
Dick Potter!
Mrs Potter I'm afraid my time is limited.
Dick (*sympathetically*) I'm sorry to hear that.

Mrs Potter hesitates then angrily gives up and heads for the dining-room. She stops in the doorway

Mrs Potter Will you kindly relay that to Mr Kerwood.
Dick Is that Bradford, Bingley or Thomas?

Mrs Potter goes to answer, gives up and storms back into the dining-room, slamming the door

The seat of the sofa springs up

Bloody hell!

Tom enters from the bedroom as:

Dick rushes to close the seat

Tom (*calling into the bedroom*) Stay in there until Mama arrives!

Dick points to the bin bag in the sofa-bed

Dick You still haven't got rid of your bits and pieces.
Tom (*furious*) I've had other things — ! (*Yelling*) They're not my bits and pieces! (*He slams the lid down*)
Dick (*placating him*) OK, OK.
Tom It's been a case of first bloody things first!
Dick You're right. Up-date!
Tom Bloody hell!
Dick If you need my assistance I need to know the porkies you've told.

Tom takes a breath

Tom (*tersely*) Your brother Harry has got himself married to some bird called Nellie and my Linda's nickname is Adriatica, which also happens to be the name I've given our illegal refugee, who that policeman thinks is my wife and whose mother has sadly died after being hit by a bus in Brixton but thank goodness the plumber is in the bedroom fixing the leak!

Dick opens his mouth to congratulate him but pauses

Dick No, you've lost me now.
Tom I'm not going through it again!

Dick's leg suddenly shoots out and starts to shake. Dick giggles and squirms for a moment while Tom watches him, bemused

Dick My mobile's on vibrate. (*He desperately tries to get his hand in his pocket. He finally gets the mobile out and presses a button. On the mobile*) Hallo? ... Do I know you, Boris?
Tom Who is it?
Dick (*to Tom*) Somebody called Boris. Got a foreign accent. ... (*On the mobile*) Oh, yeah? And what makes you think they might be here, Boris? ... I see ... (*To Tom*) He's asking about those two! (*He points upstairs*)
Tom He must have got your mobile number from Mama. Give it here!

Tom grabs the mobile from Dick

(*On the mobile, pleasantly*) Hallo, Boris! ... (*Surprised*) Oh. *You're* coming over to collect Katerina and her grandfather. Well we were actually expecting Mama or one of the family. ... I see ... You're a sort of middle man, are you? ... Have what money ready? ... Well, if that was the arrangement I'm sure either Katerina or ... yes, of course, I'll make that clear to them, Boris. No money, no delivery to Shepherd's Bush ... and they'll go back to Calais. ... Chopped up in what? ... Little bits and pieces, right. Well, it's been lovely talking to you. And may I say, Boris, how very good your English is.

An ashen Tom returns the phone to Dick

Tom (*suddenly yelling to Dick*) This is all your fault! (*Marching to* DL) Why did I listen to you? Why?!

Dick (*hurrying to Tom*) They'll have the money. They're bound to.

Behind them, a happily tipsy Andreas enters from the bedroom still with his bottle of brandy and still carrying his trumpet

Tom But what if they haven't?! We'll have two lots of bits and pieces in bin bags!

They notice Andreas and cross over to him

We want to ask you something!

Andreas Geezooar! [Cheers!] GEZUAR!

Tom Listen! You have *money* for this *Boris* bloke.

Andreas (*happily*) Geezooar! [Cheers!] GEZUAR!

Tom Money!

Dick For Boris!

Andreas (*happily*) Geezooar! [Cheers!] GEZUAR!

Tom Boris — as in Karloff!

Andreas (*to Dick*) Garloof?

Dick Boris Karloff!

Tom Karloff! Frankenstein! Monster!

Tom then mimes the Frankenstein Monster, walking in circles

Dick (*to Andreas*) Monster! (*He mimes the monster*)

Andreas (*happily*) Ah, Moonster! (*He marches to below the sofa-bed miming a monster*)

Tom (*to Andreas*) Stop that!

Katerina appears from the bedroom

Katerina (*entering*) Joosh! Koo yay? [Granddad! Where are you?] GJYSH! KU JE?

Andreas (*laughing*) Moonster! Moonster! (*He collapses on to the sofa-bed*)
Dick (*grabbing Katerina*) Katerina! Listen. (*He shows her his mobile*) Boris
— telephoned!
Katerina (*horrified, pointing*) Boreesee telefonoy! [Boris telephoned!]
BORISI TELEFONOI!
Tom Do you have *money*? (*He takes a £5 note from his pocket*) *Money* for
Boris!!
Katerina (*realizing, still scared*) Money! Boris! Yays! Yays! (*She nods her
head emphatically and then proceeds to lift her skirt*) For Boris, for Boris!
Dick Lucky old Boris.

She removes a large stuffed envelope from her drawers

Tom Thank God! You give that Boris. Boris drive you to Shepherd's Bush.
(*He mimes driving a car*)
Katerina (*alarmed*) Boris?! No! No *Boris! Mama!* (*She mimes driving a
car*) Mama brrrrrm Sheepherd's Bowsh.
Tom No, no. *Boris* come *here* for *you*.
Katerina Here?! (*To Andreas, angrily*) Hey! Boris here! (*She mimes
driving*) Brrrrrrm Sheepherd's Bowsh!
Andreas (*surprised and angry*) Boris here, Sheepherd's Bowsh! (*He does
fierce karate*)
Dick It's OK! *You* have *money*. No problem. (*He gives two thumbs up*)
Katerina Boris is ——

She spits on the floor. Tom wipes his shoe

Andreas Boris is ——

He spits. Tom wipes his shoe again

Boris is Moonster! Moonster! (*He walks in a circle as the monster which
now resembles The Hunchback of Notre-Dame*)

*Mrs Potter, clutching several papers, enters angrily shutting the door
behind her*

Mrs Potter Is there any sign of …?

*She stops on seeing Andreas beside her circling as the monster. Andreas sees
her and stops*

Andreas (*pointing to Mrs Potter*) Ah, Mrs Moonster!

Tom quickly steps in and pulls Andreas across him

Tom We're still rehearsing, Mrs Potter. Uncle Bert got a bit carried away. He's got this idea of sort of mixing his character of Titus Anute with The Hunchback of Notre-Dame — who plays the trumpet. We thought we'd go along with it, didn't we, Dick?
Dick (*correcting him*) Bingley.

Tom considers this

Tom Yes. (*To Mrs Potter*) I call Bingley Dick because he's a bit of a ——
Mrs Potter Mr Kerwood —— !
Tom Mrs Potter.
Mrs Potter It's quite apparent your rehearsal is going to conflict with our interview.
Tom No, we're just finishing! (*To Andreas*) Thanks, Uncle Bert. Well done, Uncle Bert. Off you go, Uncle Bert.
Andreas (*happily*) Unclebert-Humperdink.

Tom shoves Andreas out the way US

Dick (*referring to Katerina*) And this is Cousin Clara Humperdink who's playing Mrs Andronicus.

Katerina curtsies

Mrs Potter Mr Kerwood!
Tom Mrs Potter.
Mrs Potter If you and your wife do not start this interview within the next two minutes I'm leaving for my next appointment.
Tom Two minutes! Say goodbye, family.
Katerina Goodbye!
Dick Goodbye.

Katerina curtsies

Andreas Goodbye, Mrs Moonster. Uncle Bert Humperdink! (*He bows and falls behind the sofa*)

Mrs Potter glares at them and exits into the dining-room

Tom (*pulling Andreas to his feet*) I'll give you Engelbert Humperdink! (*To Dick*) Take them upstairs until Boris arrives! (*Opening the sofa-bed*) I'm gonna get rid of this lot.

Andreas Unclebert Humperdink! (*He raises his brandy bottle and accidentally drops the bottle into the sofa-bed. He climbs in to retrieve it*) My brandy! My brandy!
Tom Get out of there.

Tom grabs Andreas's collar and lifts him up but Andreas drops his trumpet

Andreas My trumpet! My trumpet!
Tom Come out!

He grabs Andreas

The kitchen door is suddenly pushed open by Linda

Linda All done!

But the door only opens about eight inches and hits the wheelbarrow. During the following, Linda noisily struggles to get through the kitchen door, seeing nothing of the others' activities

On hearing Linda's voice, the others freeze for a moment

Tom (*whispering urgently to Andreas*) Get back in!
Andreas (*protesting*) Eyo, eyo, eyo. [No, no, no.] JO, JO, JO.
Tom (*trying to shut the lid on Andreas*) Yes, yes, yes.
Katerina Joosh! [Granddad!] GJYSH!

She moves to help Andreas but Dick pulls her away

Dick Jooshy be OK.

Dick pulls Katerina upstairs

Andreas (*protesting*) Eyo, eyo, eyo. [No, no, no.] JO, JO, JO.
Tom (*whispering urgently*) Yes, yes, yes. Shut up! And stay in there.

He forces Andreas down into the sofa-bed. He slams the seat down

Linda Bloody wheelbarrow! (*She pushes herself through the door*)

Dick and Katerina disappear upstairs

Linda angrily pushes the wheelbarrow into the kitchen and slams the door as Tom leaps over the sofa-bed and sits. Linda turns to see Tom happily sitting there smiling at her

I thought you were sorting out the stop-cock for the plumbers.

Tom Did that. They've gone.

Linda OK! Let's go and face Mrs Potter. This is it! Come on. (*She holds out her hand and turns to the dining-room*)

Tom suddenly bounces up — Andreas has pushed up from under the seat. He bangs the seat down hard

Andreas Owww!

Linda turns at the noise and looks at Tom

Tom (*imitating Andreas*) Woowww — wow wow you look fantastic!

Linda You'd better pull yourself together before you sit down with Mrs Potter.

As she turns to the dining-room door a low sharp note is heard from Andreas's trumpet. Linda turns to look at Tom. He looks apologetic

Tom I think what Harry's got is catching.

The trumpet noise is heard again. Tom smiles apologetically

Linda Well, for God's sake don't do it in front of Mrs Potter.

An angry Mrs Potter appears in the open dining-room doorway, clutching her briefcase

Mrs Potter (*entering*) I'm sorry, Mr Kerwood — ! (*Seeing Linda*) Oh!

Tom (*still sitting happily*) Mrs Potter! Meet my wife! Mrs wife, meet my Potter!

Linda shoots him a look

Linda (*with enthusiastic agitation*) How do you do, Mrs Potter! Linda Kerwood. I *do* apologize about the confusion. Obviously our fault.

Mrs Potter moves up to get her coat followed by a distressed Linda

Mrs Potter I'm sorry, Mrs Kerwood, but I just can't wait any longer. I have to go.

Linda
Tom } (*together*) No!

Linda (*panicking*) Not without seeing us, please!

Mrs Potter I have an interview with another couple in Lambeth at 10.45. I'll be late as it is.

Linda Please!

A longer trumpet noise is heard. There is a brief pause then a surprised Mrs Potter and an embarrassed Linda turn to Tom. Tom smiles apologetically

(*To Mrs Potter*) My husband's a bit nervous.
Mrs Potter I know how he feels. We'll reschedule your appointment for a later date.
Linda But that'll take weeks. I'll make a wonderful mother, Mrs Potter.
Tom So will I, Mrs Potter!
Linda (*near to tears*) We've worked so hard on that questionnaire, haven't we, Tom?!

She pulls Tom up

Tom (*protesting*) No, I have to stay —— !

But she pulls him to Mrs Potter

Linda (*pressing on; crazily*) Ask us any questions you like!
Tom (*protesting*) I really should be sitting down for this!
Linda (*pressing on*) Electrical equipment! Saucepan handles!

The seat of the sofa-bed springs open and a furious Andreas (clutching his brandy bottle and his trumpet) staggers out. A horrified Tom and an amazed Mrs Potter see him. Andreas closes the sofa-bed as Linda presses on

Cleaning supplies! Safety locks! We know all about the different kinds of safety locks. First Aid kits ... ! (*Seeing Andreas; fading out*) Cakes. Sweet foods ... Limited to three small snacks ...

Andreas angrily approaches Tom

Andreas (*furious, miming*) Hy, tee ma vraver koaken. Tee boodahl etch mundoo! [Hey, you banged my head. You crazy fool!] HEK, TI ME VRAVE KOKEN. TI BUDALL E GMENDUR! (*In English*) You moonster! (*To Mrs Potter*) He moonster! (*To Linda*) He moonster! (*To Tom*) Me go dowter Sheepherd's Bowsh. Sheepherd's Bowsh, dowter!

He starts to go upstairs with the others watching him blankly

Katerina! Katerina! Kee-oh ershter nearshta pee e shmondo! Ma enzeer checkotoy. [This is a crazy house! Get me out of here.] KJO ESHTE NJEISHTEPI E GMENDUR! ME NXIRR QE KETEJ. Moonster! Moonster!

Andreas exits

Mrs Potter (*blankly*) That was your Uncle Bert.
Tom (*happily*) That's right.
Linda (*dumbly*) Uncle Bert?
Tom (*happily*) I'll explain later.
Mrs Potter He came out of the settee.
Tom Yes, he's acting Titus Anute.
Linda (*wide-eyed*) Uncle Bert? Tight as a newt?
Tom (*happily*) I'll explain later.
Mrs Potter But what on earth was that language he was speaking?
Tom Scottish.
Mrs Potter Scottish?!
Tom Yes. He's chucking in a bit of Macbeth. Glaswegian. (*In dreadful Scottish*) "To be or not to be that is the question, now is the winter of our discontent made glorious summer, you moonster!"
Mrs Potter (*interrupting*) Mr Kerwood!
Tom (*in dreadful Scottish*) Mrs Potter. (*Then normally*) Mrs Potter.
Mrs Potter To have that poor old man suffocating in a settee is taking your television programme too far.
Linda (*astonished*) Television programme?!
Tom (*happily, but beginning to crack*) I'll explain later!
Mrs Potter (*surprised*) Doesn't your wife know about Channel 4's Reality show?
Linda Channel 4's Reality ... ?!
Tom (*to Mrs Potter with feigned anger*) You have done it now! You've given the game away! She now knows! The whole point of this programme is that the wife of the house doesn't know! You've completely ... ! It's like *This Is Your Life* — the person doesn't know! You've absolutely ... ! It's all ...! (*Totally distraught*) They'll cancel it! That's what they'll do! I've lost my big chance to write, direct and produce! Uncle Bert's magnificent performance as Titus Anute will never be seen! It's a bloody tragedy!

He breaks down completely. Linda and Mrs Potter have been watching him with blank amazement. Tom pretends to pull himself together

I'm sorry! I'm sorry! I shouldn't have gone — it's just that, I've put so much effort into the whole ... So has Uncle Bert, of course, and Bradford and Bingley, Cousin Clara Humperdink ... (*To Linda*) I'll explain later — and now it's all over. It's all gone. (*Bravely*) No, I'm OK. I'm OK. I'm all right now. Let's forget "missed opportunity" and look to the future — our baby. Linda, take Mrs Potter into the dining-room. I will bring in the coffee and sandwiches and we can start our interview — the interview which will open up a new world for us. (*Getting emotional*) A bright new world for Linda and me — we will put behind us this winter of discontent and look forward to this glorious summer made possible by our son — or daughter.

Tom stands there for a moment then exits into the kitchen

Linda and Mrs Potter look at each other

Mrs Potter (*firmly*) My office will be in touch to arrange another appointment.

She moves to get her coat but Linda grabs her

Linda No, please!

Mrs Potter Although I have to say my initial report will be less than favourable.

Linda No, please, Mrs Potter! This morning's been a hell of a strain for Tom and me.

Mrs Potter For all of us, Mrs Kerwood.

Linda (*blocking her way*) Don't go! This baby means so much to us!

Mrs Potter (*putting her coat on*) I'm sorry, but your husband is in no fit state to deal with anything at this present time. And neither are you, Mrs Kerwood!

Linda I am, I am!

Mrs Potter Believe me, I know what you've been through this morning. Your poor mother suddenly dying like that ——

Linda (*still hysterical*) I promise you I'm totally in control. Ask me any of those safety questions. Go on! Saucepan handles! Electrical equipment! Plastic bags … (*She stops. Blankly*) My mother died.

Mrs Potter And so tragically, too.

Linda (*in disbelief*) My mother …

Mrs Potter puts her hand to her mouth

Mrs Potter Oh, my — ! I thought you knew!

She puts her briefcase on the chair DRC *and hurries to Linda*

Linda (*sitting on the sofa-bed, shocked*) Mummy — died?

Mrs Potter (*devastated*) I'm so sorry, Mrs Kerwood! (*She sits next to Linda*)

Linda But I don't … I mean she was so … I only … When did it happen?

Mrs Potter This morning. She was hit by a bus in Brixton.

Linda Ohhh!

Tom enters breezily from the kitchen with tray of sandwiches, cake, plates and cutlery

Tom Right! Coffee's nearly ready.
Mrs Potter (*appalled*) I thought your wife knew!
Tom Knew what?
Mrs Potter That her mother had died this morning.

Tom drops the tray. Mrs Potter stands up

I really do have to go now.
Tom Yes, that's probably a very good idea.

He quickly takes Mrs Potter to the front door

Mrs Potter No, no. My briefcase!
Tom You don't need your briefcase!
Mrs Potter Of course I do!
Tom I'll get it!

He quickly runs to get the briefcase as Linda comes to

Linda (*suddenly*) God! I must ring Daddy! (*She picks up the cordless phone*)
Tom No!

But she is already dialling

Linda, don't!

He moves in but Mrs Potter bars the way

Mrs Potter (*to Tom*) She naturally wants to speak to her father.
Linda (*weeping*) He'll be absolutely shattered!
Tom We all are! Bye, Mrs Potter! We'll fix another date. Next week, yeah?

He bundles the briefcase on to her and pushes her to the front door

Linda (*sobbing, on the phone*) Hallo? ... Oh, hallo, Mum!

Tom and Mrs Potter stop and slowly turn

It's me. Get Dad quick! (*She continues to sob for a moment than she stops, realizing that she's been talking to her mother. On the phone*) Hi, Dad — put Mum back on, will you? ... (*Blankly*) Mum? ... Is that you? ... You all right? … Just checking. Bye. (*She calmly switches the phone off. Then turns to Tom with growing disbelief and anger*) Why did you say Mummy had died?!!

Tom I'll explain later.

Linda Of all the cruel, heartless, wicked ——

Tom Not in front of Mrs Potter. Bye, Mrs Potter.

Linda (*on the attack, but still weeping*) Why did you tell Mrs Potter Mummy had died when you knew she hadn't! (*She slams the phone into its cradle*)

Tom No, I don't think I actually said that.

Mrs Potter You did! Hit by a bus in Brixton.

Linda (*stifling a sob*) Ohhh!

Tom (*to Mrs Potter, belligerently*) They weren't my exact words!

Mrs Potter (*fighting back*) They certainly were! You were sitting right there. You said, "My mother-in-law has died".

Linda (*stifling a sob*) Ohhh!

Tom (*to Mrs Potter, still on the attack*) It might have sounded like that.

Mrs Potter (*even stronger*) Couldn't have been more precise. You said the bus was going to Victoria.

Linda (*stifling a sob*) Ohhh!

Tom (*to Linda*) I'll explain later!

Linda No! Now! Did you tell this lady your mother-in-law had died this morning?!

Mrs Potter (*stronger than ever*) Yes he did!

Tom (*confronting Mrs Potter equally strong*) All right, I did!

Mrs Potter I told you.

Linda Why?!

Mrs Potter Yes, why?

Tom (*to Mrs Potter*) Because — she had!

Linda What?

Tom My mother-in-law had died!

Linda What the hell are you talking about?

Tom My mother-in-law! The one you don't know about! The mother of my *first* wife. Bye, Mrs Potter!

He goes to move Mrs Potter but Mrs Potter won't budge

Linda (*flabbergasted*) The mother of your first —— ?

Tom (*interrupting*) My first wife, yes. It was years before I met you. I was young. So was she. It didn't work out. Quickie divorce. There you have it.

He goes to move Mrs Potter but she won't budge

Linda (*agog*) Are you telling me —— ?

Tom (*getting hysterical*) Yes. She was from Gdansk. Ski instructress. Adriatica. She didn't speak English. I didn't speak Gdansk. I suppose that's one of the reasons it didn't work out. That and not getting enough ——

He does a quick mad pelvis mime, then realizes and grabs Mrs Potter — but she won't budge

Linda (*open mouthed*) I can't believe I'm hearing this,
Tom I can't believe I'm telling you! I should have done. I know that. Adriatica telephoned me this morning. She thought I ought to know about her mother's funeral. (*To Mrs Potter*) Her mother quite liked me!

Linda bursts into tears and runs into the bedroom

During the following speech, Mrs Potter picks up her briefcase and walks to the front door

Linda … ! (*Turning to Mrs Potter*) Mrs Potter … ! You mustn't let this jeopardize our chances with that baby! I made a mistake. I confessed. I've been a good husband, honest. And I'll be an even better Dad ——

Mrs Potter gives him a withering look and exits

He runs up into the front doorway

(*Calling*) And my Linda is a fantastic lady. She'll make the most wonderful … (*In despair he closes the door*)

Dick pops his head round from upstairs

Dick Not good, mate.

Tom looks at him

I liked the mother-in-law being hit by a 34 bus. But not good, mate.
Tom (*flatly*) I've lost us the chance of a baby.
Dick There'll be a next time.
Tom No, I've lost our baby, I'm stuck with two illegal immigrants, my wife's going to kill me, there's a suspicious copper out the back and any minute now Boris will arrive. (*He spits on the floor*)
Dick It can only get better.
Tom (*suddenly*) I'm going to tell Linda the truth! And everybody else!
Dick (*worried*) What?

Tom The immigrants. The body parts. I should never have listened to you two in the first place. (*He opens the sofa-bed and starts to pull out the bin bag*) Give us a hand to get this lot out.

Dick (*going to the sofa-bed*) Tom, stop and think! Those illegal refugees!

Tom We'll hand them over. They'll go through the due process.

Dick No, think for a moment — what those two have been through to get here. We'll never know, mate. You saw Katerina when she was talking to her mum on the phone. Yeah! Never mind the fags and the brandy and Harry's car and this poor old fart (*he points to the sofa-bed*) — those two refugees are going to be re-united with their *family*. They might not get away with it. But they've risked their lives for this chance of freedom.

Tom (*determined*) I'm sorry, Dick!

Dick And then what will this Boris bloke do to you?

There is a brief pause

Tom You're right! (*He throws the bin liner back into the sofa-bed and slams the seat down*)

The kitchen door opens and Downs backs in

Tom and Dick quickly sit innocently on the sofa-bed and smile at Downs

Downs (*talking off*) I said no!!

Harry hurriedly enters from the kitchen

Harry (*entering*) I really think it's worth it, Officer!

During the following, Downs closes the kitchen door, puts his finger on Harry's chest and sits him with Tom and Dick

Downs No, *Bradford*! I am not going to look through all your brother's dustbins for his tax disc! (*To Tom*) Now I reckon you and your two little playmates — Bradford and Bingley — are up to something more interesting than unpaid tax discs. So what little game are we playing, eh?

Dick and Harry go into pat-a-cake, pat-a-cake routine

Don't you be funny with me!

The bedroom door opens and a determined but still tearful Linda appears carrying a packed suitcase. She slams the door shut and heads towards the front door

Tom rises, goes to her and pushes her past the front door to DL

Tom Linda —— !
Linda I'll be in touch.
Tom Linda, darling! What're you doing? Where you going?
Linda To stay with Mum and Dad for a couple of days.
Tom You don't have to do that!
Linda I need to sort myself out. (*She moves past Tom but stops on seeing Downs*) You're a policeman.
Downs Yes, madam! May I ask who you are?
Linda I'm Mrs Kerwood.
Downs So you're Nellie, are you?
Linda Nellie?
Downs Married to Bradford here. (*He points to Harry*)
Linda Bradford?!
Tom She's not married to Bradford.
Harry (*rising*) And Bingley's not married.
Dick (*rising*) No, I'm not married.
Downs Shut up!

They sit

Linda Bingley?!
Downs (*pointing to Dick and Harry on the sofa-bed*) Look, which one of these two jokers are you married to?
Linda (*pointing to Tom*) Him.
Downs (*confused*) No, no. I met that one's wife earlier, right here.
Linda You what?
Tom That was my first wife! I told you about Adriatica.
Downs (*surprised*) Your first wife?

Harry and Dick rise

Harry They're divorced now.
Dick Divorced now.
Downs Shut up!

They sit

Linda (*agog*) What was your first wife doing here?
Tom Visiting.
Linda Visiting?
Downs No, No, you said it was Uncle Bert who was visiting, having a break from Auntie Flo.

Linda Never mind Uncle Bert and … ! (*She stops*) Auntie Flo?
Dick (*rising*) Yeah, after fifty years Uncle Bert walked out on her. He woke up this morning and said, "Sorry, I'm going to scarper Flo!"
Downs Shut it!

Dick sits. Harry rises

Harry He left without a penny, too. So he had to phone her up and say, "Could you let me have some cash, Flo!"
Downs Belt up!

Harry sits

Linda (*to Tom*) Look, I don't give a damn about those bloody relations of yours, why were you seeing this Adriatica woman in our house?
Dick He was consoling her because her mother had just been hit by a 34 bus going to Victoria.

Dick rises

Downs Shut it.

Dick sits

Tom (*to Linda*) Darling! Adriatica was in and out in half a minute.
Downs No, no, I bumped into her twice.
Linda Twice?!
Downs (*to Linda*) The second time he was shoving Adriatica back in the bedroom.
Linda (*staggered*) The bedroom?!

Dick and Harry rise

Dick
Harry } (*together*) We can explain that as well.
Downs Sit!

They sit

Downs And stay.
Linda First of all you keep this first wife of yours a secret. Now I find you're snogging her in our bedroom!

She storms to the front door and opens it. Tom hurries after her

Tom Linda! Hold it! She's not really ... ! (*He stops*)

Linda turns in the open doorway. Tom hesitates and quickly looks to Dick,
then to Downs, then upstairs, then back to Linda

Linda Not really *what*?
Tom Not really as nice as you.
Linda But better in bed, yeah?!
Tom Yes. No!
Linda (*nearly breaking up*) I think it's just as well we didn't get that baby.

Linda runs out weeping

Tom Linda ... !

There is a pause

Harry (*to Dick*) I didn't know the 34 bus went to Victoria.
Downs (*to Tom*) Looks as though having no tax disc is the least of your
    problems. Right. I've got all your details, Mr Kerwood. You'll be receiving
    a summons in due course regarding the tax disc.
Tom (*flatly*) Yeah. Have a nice day.
Downs Don't worry, I've got a feeling I'll be back. Gardeners, ex-wives,
    Titus Anute. (*To Dick*) He must think I'm a perfect idiot.
Dick Nobody's perfect, Constable.

Downs doesn't react and turns to the front door to exit

Mrs Potter storms in. She is nearly cracking up by now

Tom Mrs Potter, you're back!
Mrs Potter Somebody is blocking my exit!
Downs I beg your pardon ... ?
Mrs Potter My car is stuck between a white van and some kind of station
    wagon. I've been trying to manoeuvre out for the last five minutes.
Tom No problem. The white van's mine. Bingley! You've got the keys.
Dick Yes, sir. Kerwood, Mr Brother, sir! (*He rises and moves to the front*
    door. To Harry) Don't you move, Brother Bradford! We don't want
    anything else popping up. (*To Downs*) Constable. (*To Mrs Potter*)
    Gainsborough.

Dick smiles and exits through the front door

Mrs Potter (*to Downs*) The driver of the station wagon was most unhelpful. I asked him if he'd kindly back up a yard or two and he just sat behind his wheel and gave me a gesture with his finger that I'd never seen before.

Harry You don't mean he … (*He gives a rude gesture with his middle finger*)

Mrs Potter That's right.

Downs (*looking at Tom*) I know how he feels.

Downs exits through the front door

Tom While you're here, Mrs Potter. Have a cup of tea and we can discuss ——

Mrs Potter (*getting hysterical*) I don't want a cup of anything, thank you! I want to get out of this madhouse and on to my next appointment!

Dick hurries in through the open front door

Dick There's been a development!

Mrs Potter (*tersely*) Have you moved Mr Kerwood's van?

Dick No, I was delayed by the driver of the station wagon.

Mrs Potter Did he give *you* a rude gesture, too?

Dick (*moving to Tom*) No. (*Pointedly*) He's actually called to collect something of ours, Tom. (*Pointing outside*) Mr Boris!

Tom Thank God! Sheepherd's Bowsh.

Mrs Potter (*to Dick*) In the meantime perhaps you'll move your van in order to unblock my exit.

Dick (*to Mrs Potter*) You move it, will you, love? Leave the keys in the van.

Dick throws the keys to a surprised Mrs Potter and moves to Tom

Mrs Potter (*to Dick*) Bingley!

Dick turns to Mrs Potter who angrily gives the finger gesture

Mrs Potter storms out slamming the door behind her

During the following, Tom opens the sofa-bed and starts to remove the bin bag

Dick I don't like the look of this Boris bloke!

Tom He's lovely. He's getting rid of our bloody immigrants. (*To Harry*) You! Get the wheelbarrow.

Harry I still think we can bury him in the ——

Tom Get the —— !

Harry Get the bloody wheelbarrow, right.

Harry hurriedly exits into the kitchen

Tom (*to Dick*) And you — !
Dick The bloody immigrants, right.

Dick hurries upstairs as Harry returns with the wheelbarrow

During the following, Tom and Harry remove the bin bag from the sofa-bed

Harry Look, if you don't want to bury it, let's try Alfie's idea ——
Tom (*interrupting*) You'll get something buried in the back of your head, Harry! Now for the last time! (*He slams the sofa-bed shut*)

They throw the bin bag into the wheelbarrow

Harry The Clapham dump, OK. (*Looking at the bin bag in the* wheelbarrow) I wonder what this poor bloke did when he was all in one piece?

Tom slowly turns

I mean, to end up with sections in a bin liner with four Sainsbury bags in a wheelbarrow ——

Tom is looking at him expressionlessly

— the Clapham dump.

Harry hurries into the kitchen with the wheelbarrow as Dick hurries on from the upstairs landing leading Katerina by the hand. Katerina is wearing her holdall once again

Dick Granddad's on his way and I've given the lovely Katerina my telephone numbers, haven't I, darlin'?
Katerina (*holding up a piece of paper; in English*) Telephone for Dick.
Dick That's all you have to do, yeah! Remember that's my flat number.
Katerina OK!
Dick And that's my mobile.
Katerina You mobile.
Dick Oh, very! (*To Tom*) We're going to meet up so she can teach me to speak Albanian.
Tom You can't even speak English, you muppet.

Katerina Hey, hey. Dick-nice-man.
Dick (*to Tom*) See, Dick nice man. You, Moonster. (*He does a Karloff walk*)

Andreas appears on the stairs carrying several cartons of cigarettes. He is once more wearing his haversack

Andreas (*seeing Dick*) Ah, Moonster! Garloof! (*He turns to do Karloff walk and drops the cigarettes, sending them flying*)
Katerina Joosh! [Granddad!] GJYSH!

She and Dick rush to help Andreas. During the following, they fill his haversack with the cartons of cigarettes

Tom Just get them out of here.
Dick Upsa-daisy. Upsa-daisy.
Andreas Oopsa-dicey, oopsa-dicey.
Katerina (*putting the cigarettes in his haversack*) Yar koo ee kay cigaret. [Here's your cigarettes.] JA KU I KE CIGARETTE.
Dick (*to Andreas*) You OK. now.
Andreas OK. Dykie boy!
Dick Bye-bye Jooshy.
Tom Come on! They've got Boris waiting out there. Bye-bye, Granddad Humperdink!

They shake hands

Andreas (*laughing*) Bye-bye, Mr Moonster!

Tom shakes Katerina's hand

Katerina Thank you, thank you!
Tom Bye, bye, Katerina Adriatica Armenia cousin Clara Humperdink!

Katerina kisses Tom's hand

Katerina (*to Dick*) Bye-bye — Tricky Dicky.
Dick (*to Tom*) I taught her to say that. (*To Katerina*) Bye-bye, lovely granddaughter.

Dick holds out his hand. She grabs him and hugs him

   (*His leg starting to vibrate again*) It's not the mobile this time.
Tom Time to go!

They start to move US. *Tom opens the front door*

> *Boris is revealed. He enters and closes the front door behind him. Boris is a stocky East-European about forty, very smartly dressed and carrying a briefcase. He is very businesslike. He speaks perfect English but with a strong accent*

> *As he purposefully walks in between them, Katerina and Andreas break to below the sofa-bed with Katerina pulling Andreas behind her to protect him*

Dick (*nervously*) It's all right, Boris, they're coming! Oh — you haven't met my brother, Tom, have you? Tom — Boris, Boris — Tom.
Boris I don't have much time, Mr Kerwood, but it's a pleasure to meet you.

Boris shakes hands with Tom which practically kills Tom

Tom (*trying to cover his nervousness*) Likewise. Mr — er —— ?
Boris Mr Anaroskipetrivisnikotch.

For a brief moment Tom considers the lengthy name

Tom Likewise, Boris.
Boris (*to Katerina, with a big smile*) Katerina! Nice to see you. Pershendatia! [Greetings!] PERSHENDETJE!

She doesn't answer

I trust you had a pleasant journey from Calais.

She doesn't answer

Boris (*big smile*) Andreas! Long time no see. Pershendatia! [Greetings!] PERSHENDETJE!

Andreas spits on the ground. Boris's smile vanishes and he raises his hand to attack Andreas

Tom (*quickly*) Boris, I think he's got a touch of catarrh.
Boris (*to Katerina*) So — the money. Quick! English pounds we said, yeah! Poundet oonglez. [English pounds.] PAUNDET ANGLEZ.

Katerina nods. Boris holds out his hand. Katerina hesitates then turns her back and starts to get the envelope from beneath her dress

Dick I'm going to buy her a handbag for Christmas.

Katerina hands the money to Boris who has put his briefcase on the sofa-bed. He puts the money in and takes out several passports. He selects two and throws the others back. He then offers one passport to Katerina. She grabs it and holds out her hand for the other passport. Boris smiles and holds out his other hand. Katerina looks confused

Tom Problem?
Boris (*to Tom*) I want another four thousand pounds. (*To Katerina*) Nae tjeter katermeesha Katerina. [Another four thousand.] NJE TJETER KATER-MIJESHE.
Katerina Eyo! Eyo! Eyo!! Tee the katermee per doo — [No! No, no. You said four thousand for two —] JO! JO, JO. TI THE KATERMIJE PER DY — (*she holds up two fingers*) — passaporta. [— passports.] — PASAPORTA.
Boris (*shaking his head, still polite*) No, no, no! Katermee per atter passaport. [Four thousand for that passport.] KATERMIJE PER ATE PASAPORTE. (*He points to the one she's holding*) The katermee per cutter passaport. [And four thousand for this passport.] DHE KATERM-IJE PER KETE PASAPORTE. (*He holds up the one he's holding*)
Katerina Eyo! [No!] JO!
Andreas (*to Katerina*) Chfara po tote? [What's he saying?] CFARE PO THOTE?
Katerina Doe ma shoomar parra. [He wants more money.] DO ME SHUME PARA.
Andreas Ma shooma parra?! Eyo! [More money?! No!] ME SHUME PARA?! JO! (*To Boris*) Moonster!

Andreas spits on the ground. Boris's smile vanishes and he raises his hand to strike Andreas

Dick (*quickly*) Boris. Do you have a fisherman's friend? Probably not.
Boris (*to Katerina*) So four thousand katermee. [Four thousand.] KATER-MIJE.
Tom (*to Boris, politely*) Excuse me.

Boris turns to him, deadpan

(*Stepping to Boris, putting his hand in his trouser pocket*) Would you settle for ten quid now and the rest over ——
Boris (*whipping out a gun*) Get back!

Tom quickly steps back. Boris turns to Katerina and Andreas pointing the gun. Katerina steps in front of Andreas to protect him. Tom steps behind Dick

The kitchen door opens and Harry comes in pushing the wheelbarrow with the bin liner

Harry Would you bloody believe it, the bloody car won't start ... ! (*He stops on seeing the scene*) Ooh!

Tom (*with false brightness*) Harry! (*Babbling on nervously to Boris*) This is my younger brother, Harry. Oo! You didn't actually get a formal introduction to Dick did you. Richard! Tricky Dicky as he's known in the family. (*To Harry, indicating Boris*) And this gentleman is (*he mumbles something vaguely Russian which finishes with*) scratchbollockoff. And — er — there appears to be a slight problem about the cost of the transaction.

Boris (*pointing the gun at Tom's mouth*) Shut up! (*To Katerina*) No money — no passport. No Shepherd's Bush. (*He throws the passport back into the briefcase*)

Katerina (*frightened*) No Sheepherd's Bowsh!

Boris Back to *Kosova*, yeah?!

Katerina Kosova, No!

Andreas Kosova?!

Tom Boris, I don't think they fancy Kosova.

Boris (*big smile*) Yes! Kosova. Home.

Dick I think they wanted to make a home here, actually.

Boris (*grimly*) Then I want another four thousand pounds.

Boris suddenly makes a lunge for Katerina who has got her hand in her holdall. He grabs her hand, twists it violently and her knife falls to the ground. Boris quickly picks it up

(*To Katerina, as to a naughty schoolgirl*) Little girls shouldn't play with sharp knives.

Tom (*without thinking*) Do you know that's the first rule on the adoption paper.

Boris Shut up! They either give me more money or they go back home — (*pointing the knife at Katerina and Andreas*) — in instalments. (*He flicks the knife up and down*)

Tom } (*together*) { But they don't have any money!
Dick } { They've already given you the lot!

Boris Back!

Harry (*largely*) Hang on a second! Hold it, hold it, hold it!

Harry confronts Tom and Dick

Is this all over four thousand nicker? Is it? Are you risking their two lives 'cos of a measly four thousand. You miserable penny-pinching pair of scum-bags. Give it to him. Yeah! You two. Give Boris his four thousand quid.

Tom ⎱ (*together, confused*) When you say give it to him ...?!
Dick ⎰

Harry Yeah! From that lot. (*He points to the bin liner in the wheelbarrow*)

They all look. Tom and Dick look blankly back to Harry

Yeah! (*To Boris*) There's more than two hundred thousand there if you take into account their cocaine racket and the fake IDs.

Boris stares at Harry. Harry doesn't flinch. Boris hesitates then walks over to the bin liner. At the same time Boris indicates for all of them to move over to below the sofa-bed

Go on, Boris. Never mind the four thousand. Take the lot.

During the following, Boris heaves the bin liner from the wheelbarrow and dumps it on the ground. He then points the gun at them and indicates for all of them to sit down on the sofa-bed. Boris puts the gun on the arm of the chair then holds the top of the bin liner up and inserts the knife in the top of the plastic. He gives a rip — puts the knife on the table R of the chair and then opens the bin bag wide

You've earned it, mate. All kinds of currencies there. Pounds, dollars, euros, kroner. All nicely wrapped up. Go on. Help yourself! Go on. Take your pound of flesh!

Tom and Dick now realize what Harry is up to. Boris hesitates for a moment then puts his head into the bin-liner. His head immediately shoots out again

Boris (*reacting to the stench*) Corrrrrr!

Dick and Katerina leap forward and thrust Boris's head back in the bin bag with Andreas screaming. Tom and Harry quickly lift the bin bag up over Boris's head so that he is standing upright with the bin bag covering him. Andreas gives Tom his long waist-scarf which Tom ties round the bin bag at Boris's waist to secure it. Boris is yelling and staggering around while everyone else is screaming triumphantly, Harry is now going into a warm-up karate routine to deliver the coup de grâce to Boris

Downs comes through the front door, into the pandemonium

No-one sees him

Harry Ahhhh — so!

Harry kicks the head of the staggering bin bag who collapses into the arms of Tom and Dick who ease the unconscious Boris into the wheelbarrow. The victorious group are congratulating each other as Andreas plays "Rule Britannia" on his trumpet. Downs walks behind the sofa-bed to DR. *Harry is celebrating by doing more karate exercises as the others see Downs. They all subside except Harry who continues doing violent karate chops in the air*

Harry (*happily*) Ee-ee-ee! Ee-ee-ee!!

Harry sees Downs who is surveying Harry po-faced

(*Unhappily*) Ee-ee-evening all!
Downs (*levelly*) I'd come back to tell you that Mrs Potter lady has severely damaged your van and a station wagon while trying to get out. And in damaging your van a number of those aforementioned boxes had spilled open revealing a quantity of cigarettes and brandy. (*He pauses*) That's what I'd come back to tell you. (*He pauses*) However … (*He points to the bin liner*) The case of the cavorting bin liner. (*He smiles dangerously at them*) You three! Messrs Thomas, Bradford and Bingley Kerwood!

Downs beckons Tom, Dick and Harry who line up

OK! (*To Tom*) You first.

Tom steps forward

(*Pointing to the bin liner*) Who's that in there?
Tom That, Constable, is a very dangerous bloke who was threatening us with that gun there.

Dick takes the gun (by the muzzle) from the arm of the chair and passes it to Downs

Dick (*stepping forward*) Which will have his fingerprints on it. As will that briefcase which contains several fake British passports.

Downs places the gun (by the muzzle) in the briefcase

Harry (*stepping forward*) And I bet you'll find names of accomplices in there as well. Probably a diary, too. His name's Boris by the way.

Downs Boris?

Tom I reckon you might have caught yourself a big fish there, Officer.

Downs Wait a minute. Did you say Boris?

Tom ⎫   ⎧ Yeah, that's right, Boris.
Dick ⎬ (*together*) ⎨ Boris, yeah.
Harry ⎭   ⎩ That's him, Boris.

They all spit on the ground

Downs But, blimey, it's not ...?! I mean it can't be ... Boris Anaroskipetrivisnikotch.

Tom, Dick and Harry all look surprised

Tom ⎫   ⎧ Yeah, that's the bloke. Boris Anaroskicutyerbollockoff.
Dick ⎬ (*together*) ⎨ Yeah, that's the bloke. Boris Anaroskigotyerfingeroff.
Harry ⎭   ⎩ Yeah, that's the bloke. Boris Anaroskiknockyertopperoff.

They spit on the ground

Downs Boris Anaroskipetrivisnikotch is the top man in the East European Mafia!

Tom ⎫   ⎧ Top man, eh?! Boris Anaroskicutyerbollockoff.
Dick ⎬ (*together*) ⎨ What do you know! Boris Anaroskigotyerfingeroff.
Harry ⎭   ⎩ Is that a fact?! Boris Anaroskiknockyertopperoff.

They spit on the ground. Downs moves DL to inspect the bin liner in the wheelbarrow

Downs Bloody hell, who'd have thought it. Boris Anaroskipetrivisnikotch.

Dick (*impressed*) He gets it right every time, doesn't he?

Downs starts to take notes while looking at the bin liner

Tom Constable, will it be OK for Uncle Bert to take my ex-wife home?

Downs Providing neither of them was witness to any of this. (*He points to the bin liner*)

Tom No, definitely not. They didn't see a thing.

Downs They can go then.

As Tom beckons Andreas and Katerina across to the sofa-bed, Downs goes back to writing down the evidence

Tom Off you go then, Uncle Bert. And by the way, you dropped this.

Tom passes Andreas the second passport which he takes from the briefcase

Andreas Oh, thank you. Thank you!

Andreas clutches the passport to his bosom as Tom neatly removes the envelope from the briefcase

Tom And Adriatica. Here's the money for the taxi to Shepherd's Bush.
Katerina (*wide-eyed*) Taxi, Sheepherd's Bowsh?!
Tom (*thrusting money on her*) You've got to tip the driver as well, you know.
Katerina (*laughing*) No Moonster!

Laughing and crying, she hugs him. Downs looks up

Dick (*to Downs*) I think his ex is still in love with him, you know.
Katerina Bye-bye, Hairy. Bye-bye, Dickie.

Katerina quickly kisses Harry and hugs Dick

Dick (*to Downs*) Got a soft spot for her in-laws as well.

Tom sweeps Andreas and Katerina to the front door. Andreas stops and goes into a grand farewell speech

Andreas (*to Tom*) Bye-bye Moonster. (*To Harry and Dick*) Bye-bye Hairy
   Dickie. (*Nobly*) You Britaniccut yenee yamreckuluesham. Koo eshter
   deeta ma e loomtour e yetus seema. Zoltee choft mayo! [You British are
   wonderful. This is the happiest day of my life. God bless you!] JU
   BRITANIKEY JENI TE MRE KULLUESHEM. KJO ESHTE DITA ME
   E LUMTURE JETES SIME. ZOTI QOFTE ME JU!

Downs is bemused. There is an awkward silence

Tom Uncle Bert is a professor of languages at Cambridge.
Dick Yeah. That was Albanian for "I'm glad you've caught that rotten
   bastard, Boris Anaroskipetrivisnikotch." (*Realizing*) I said it!
Tom So that wraps up the case, yes, Constable.
Downs I do have one *little* question, sir.
Tom Oh, yeah?
Downs What's Boris Anaroskipetrivisnikotch doing in your living-room in
   a bin bag?
Tom I thought you said it was a little question.

Downs And do you have an answer?

Tom opens his mouth but is lost for words

Dick That's down to me. I borrowed Tom's van to go to Calais for the weekend and while I was in a café, would you believe it, the car was nicked! (*Dramatically*) Obviously by this Boris bloke. He went and filled it with all that contraband stuff, didn't he? Then he saw Tom's log book and insurance thing in the glove compartment and turned up here.
Downs Why?

Dick goes to speak then looks hopefully to Tom

Dick (*to Tom*) Back to you, Tom.
Tom (*dramatically*) He said he was looking for a safe house.
Downs For what?
Tom Well, apart from the cigarettes and brandy — he said he also smuggled illegal immigrants into this country.
Harry (*worried*) Hang on, are you sure —— ?
Tom (*interrupting*) I'm positive. (*To Downs*) Boris said he'd pay us a fortune if we'd act as a sort of half-way house. (*To Dick and Harry, outraged*) We refused, of course, didn't we?
Dick ⎫ (*together, outraged*) ⎧ Definitely, That's illegal!!
Harry ⎭ ⎩ We're law-abiding citizens!!
Tom Now, there are some *other* contents in that bin bag — which Boris brought with him from Calais. He never showed us what it was — but he *hinted* that one of his illegals hadn't paid up so …

Tom picks up Katerina's knife by its tip and offers it to Downs. Downs takes out his handkerchief and gingerly takes the knife by the blade

Downs (*aghast*) You don't mean he … ? (*He looks at the knife and mimes chopping*)
Tom We've got no proof, mind! We haven't actually seen what's in there — but he gave a *big hint*, didn't he? (*He turns to Dick and Harry*)
Dick ⎫ (*together*) Big big hint!
Harry ⎭

Downs picks up the briefcase by its edges

Downs Right! Let's get this evidence gathered up. (*He puts the briefcase in the wheelbarrow*) I'll take this criminal down to the station. (*He starts to push the wheelbarrow to the kitchen*)

Tom (*surprised*) What, like that?

Downs I want to get there before he comes to. Boris, that is, not the — er ... (*He mimes chopping*)

Tom ⎱
Dick ⎰ (*together, quickly*) No, no, no, no.
Harry ⎰

Downs I tell you. Our sergeant's going to get a surprise when he opens this lot up.

Tom ⎱   ⎧ Definitely!
Dick ⎰ (*together*) ⎨ You're right there!
Harry ⎰   ⎩ Too true!

Downs (*seriously*) And I want to commend you three for your support of the law today.

Tom ⎱   ⎧ It was nothing.
Dick ⎰ (*together*) ⎨ Think nothing of it.
Harry ⎰   ⎩ Least we could do.

Downs That's what this community needs, more honest people around like you.

Downs pushes the wheelbarrow into the kitchen and exits

Tom closes the kitchen door. There is a momentary pause then the three brothers react in their different ways

Tom (*dejected*) Oh — my ... ! (*He sits in the armchair with his head in his hands*)

Dick Wahoo! (*He bangs his fist repeatedly skywards in celebration*)

Harry Ha-ha! (*He does a celebratory jig*)

Dick (*to Tom, laughing*) You are the best lying bastard in the family!

Harry (*to Tom, laughing*) He hasn't *joined* the club, he's the bloody *president!*

Tom looks at them

Tom (*flatly*) I lost Linda and me the chance of a baby today. And I've lost Linda as well.

During the following, Linda enters behind them. She looks bedraggled and her right arm is in a sling. She walks down to them

Dick (*consoling Tom*) Yeah, well ...

Harry (*consoling Tom*) You'll get another chance, mate.

Tom Not with Mrs Potter.

Dick There are *other* agencies!
Harry Yeah. You'll be OK!

They see Linda

Tom (*referring to her arm*) Sweetheart — !
Dick   } (*together*) Linda!
Harry
Linda (*suddenly crying*) I got hit by a bicycle!
Tom (*rushing over to her*) Linda, baby! My little girl!

As he takes Linda to the sofa-bed and they sit he indicates for Dick and Harry to leave

Dick Yeah, well. Sorry about the arm, Linda. (*Trying to be funny*) This will cheer you up, did you hear about the shipload of blue paint that collided with the shipload of red paint? All the sailors got marooned.

She cries

Dick runs upstairs

Harry Hey, this will cheer you up, Linda, did you hear about the dyslexic who walked into a bra?

Tom looks at him menacingly

Well, there was this dyslexic who walked into a bra …

Tom stands and steps to Harry

Taking the hint, Harry takes a run and dives through the window

There is a crash from the dustbins

Tom (*to Linda*) You tell me all about it!
Linda (*still crying*) Well, I was upset about you and your ex-wife ——
Tom Yes, I'm going to explain about that and Uncle Bert and everything.
Linda — and I was walking to the underground and this bloke on a bicycle — (*wailing*) bumped into meeeeee!
Tom There, there!

Linda tries to pull herself together

Linda This very helpful lady — took me to the doctor's ——
Tom (*quietly*) I'm sorry, sweetheart. About cocking it up today. I know what that baby meant to you.

Linda looks at him and bursts into tears

I can't bear to see you so unhappy!
Linda (*crying*) I'm not unhappy. I'm bloody happy! (*She cries more*)
Tom (*starting to cry*) Why are you crying if you're bloody happy?
Linda (*wailing*) Because I was sick all over the doctor.
Tom (*crying*) It's been a stressful day for you.
Linda (*wailing*) No, the doctor says it's morning sickness, I'm pregnant. (*She continues to weep*)

He looks blank for a moment, then they stand up. During the following, the music starts and builds

Tom
Linda } (*together*) We're having a baby!

They laugh and hug

Linda (*yelling in pain*) Ooh. My arm!
Tom I'm sorry, darling! (*He hugs her again*)
Linda (*yelling in pain*) Ahhh!
Tom Sorry, sweetheart.

They are both laughing and crying as ——

——*the* CURTAIN *falls*

FURNITURE AND PROPERTY LIST

ACT I

On stage: Sofa-bed. *On it*: cushions
Small table L of sofa-bed. *On it*: cordless phone
Armchair. *On it*: cushions
Small table R of armchair
Desk
Coat hooks by front door. *On one*: **Linda**'s coat
Practical clock on wall
Window closed
Keys in kitchen and bedroom doors onstage side

Off stage: Official-looking document, pen (**Linda**)
Towel (**Tom**)
2 mugs of tea (**Linda**)
Shirt (**Tom**)
Tie (**Tom**)
Handbag containing purse (**Linda**)
4 full Sainsbury carrier bags. *In first*: old World War II army jacket. *In second*: 2 lemons and large packet of salt. *In third and fourth*: wrapped body parts (**Harry**)
Large unmarked box (**Dick**)
Large bunch of flowers, 2 Tesco shopping bags (**Linda**)
Second large (different shape to first) unmarked box (**Dick**)
Flowers in vase (**Linda**)
Large, heavy duty bin liner full of wrapped body parts, including head and a foot (**Harry**)
Bottle of tomato ketchup (**Linda**)
Tatty piece of paper (**Dick**)
Tray containing folded tablecloth, crockery, cutlery (**Linda**)
Packed holdall, long-bladed knife (**Katerina**)
Old haversack (**Andreas**)
Trumpet, open bottle of brandy (**Andreas**)
Thick sandwich (**Katerina**)
Wheelbarrow (**Harry**)
Half-empty bottle of brandy (**Andreas**)
Briefcase (**Mrs Potter**)

Personal **Tom**: handkerchief
Dick: car keys, mobile phone in pocket
Harry: sheaf of papers (property guide)
Downs: notebook, pen

ACT II

Re-set: Wall clock to time shown at end of Act I

Check: No key in kitchen door

Off stage: Large bin liner, 2 aerosol air fresheners (**Harry**)
              Quarter-full bottle of brandy (**Andreas**)
              Office file (**Mrs Potter**)
              Front doorkey (**Linda**)
              Several papers (**Mrs Potter**)
              Briefcase (**Mrs Potter**)
              Tray of sandwiches, cake, plates and cutlery (**Tom**)
              Packed suitcase (**Linda**)
              Holdall containing large knife (**Katerina**)
              Haversack (containing trumpet), several cartons of cigarettes (**Andreas**)
              Briefcase containing several passports (**Boris**)

Personal   **Tom**: £5 note in pocket
              Katerina: large stuffed envelope
              Dick: car keys, mobile phone
              Boris: gun
              Linda: armsling

LIGHTING PLOT

Property fittings required: nil
Interior. The same scene throughout

ACT I

To open: Full general interior lighting

Cue 1   They turn to **Mrs Potter**, each holding a body part   (Page 52)
             Black-out

ACT II

To open: Full general interior lighting

Cue 2   **Tom** and **Linda** are both laughing and crying   (Page 102)
             Black-out

EFFECTS PLOT

ACI I

Cue 1	They laugh and hug *Kettle whistles from kitchen*	(Page 2)
Cue 2	**Linda** moves towards the bedroom *Doorbell*	(Page 5)
Cue 3	**Harry** exits *Loud crash of someone falling into galvanized dustbins*	(Page 25)
Cue 4	**Tom**: " ... you cheeky bugger!" *Doorbell*	(Page 30)
Cue 5	**Tom**: " Harry! Harry!" *Doorbell*	(Page 31)
Cue 6	**Tom** turns Linda towards the kitchen *Doorbell*	(Page 31)
Cue 7	**Linda**: "Give me five minutes." *Doorbell*	(Page 32)
Cue 8	**Tom**: " ... lock door with key." *Doorbell rings insistently*	(Page 32)
Cue 9	**Tom**: " ... Mrs Potter's sandwiches." *Cordless phone rings*	(Page 46)
Cue 10	They turn to **Mrs Potter**, each holding a body part *Music*	(Page 52)

ACI I

Cue 11	**Tom** moves **Mrs Potter** towards the dining-room *Cordless phone*	(Page 56)
Cue 12	They shake **Tom**'s hand and pat him on the back *Doorbell*	(Page 58)

Cue 13	**Tom** mimes vomiting *Doorbell rings urgently*	(Page 59)
Cue 14	**Harry** dives through the window *Crash from the dustbins*	(Page 101)
Cue 15	**Tom** and **Linda** stand up *Music starts and builds*	(Page 102)

Lightning Source UK Ltd.
Milton Keynes UK
UKHW01f2000010518
321952UK00007B/210/P